The Ten Commandments
of Quality Management

The Ten Commandments of Quality Management

✦

Best Practices to Develop New Leaders and Create a Quality Environment

Ajit Silva

iUniverse, Inc.
New York Lincoln Shanghai

The Ten Commandments of Quality Management
Best Practices to Develop New Leaders and Create a Quality Environment

iUniverse books may be ordered through booksellers or by contacting:

iUniverse
2021 Pine Lake Road, Suite 100
Lincoln, NE 68512
www.iuniverse.com
1-800-Authors (1-800-288-4677)

ISBN-13: 978-0-595-35756-7 (pbk)
ISBN-13: 978-0-595-80611-9 (cloth)
ISBN-13: 978-0-595-80232-6 (ebk)
ISBN-10: 0-595-35756-3 (pbk)
ISBN-10: 0-595-80611-2 (cloth)
ISBN-10: 0-595-80232-X (ebk)

Printed in the United States of America

Dedicated to my wife Neluka,
son Tyler,
and to those who desire to be quality managers

Contents

Preface

I have been studying and practicing quality management (the style of management that emphasizes employees, customers, and owners) since 1985 and was fascinated by reading such books as *In Search of Excellence*[1], *Moments of Truth*[2], and *The Fifth Discipline*[3], and how the management of some organizations have used these principles to considerably raise employee morale, reduce attrition, increase productivity, and increase customer satisfaction, resulting in an increase in corporate profits.

Quality management was developed by Dr. W. Edwards Deming in the 1950s, but was not accepted widely in the United States. He took these principles to Japan, and the Japanese used these concepts to become economically superior. The quality movement made a big comeback in the late 1970s and early 1980s, but did not make such a big impact on the world as it should have from such books as I have mentioned above. In fact, ninety-five percent of the companies in the world today either don't practice quality management or practice it sparingly.

Why wouldn't a corporation practice behaviors that would bring it profitability? It is due to the traditional management philosophies that have been around since the beginning of time. If you are unfamiliar with what I am referring to, it is also known as the military system whose primary objective is the use of power over subjects to make them conform to a certain type of behavior. This does not mean that everyone who has served in the military acts in this manner, but is meant to characterize the behavior patterns.

When you think about it, this type of conformity and its accompanying behavior is a necessity in the military, because one has to be assured during a war that the individual standing next to you takes appropriate action for your protection and for the good of the unit. However, when this management style is transferred into the corporate environment, it removes any free thought, creativity, empowerment, and outside-the-box thinking. In fact, traditional managers punish employees for doing things other than what they are directed to do, even if it is beneficial to the corporation.

Now think about the employees in the corporate world who are stifled in this type of environment, among them scientists who are not inventing anything, and the impact that has on corporate profits. What type of behavior do you think is rewarded in these companies? The individuals that are promoted and succeed in these corporations have been mentored to act exactly as their traditional management, not to question anything, or make any effort to improve the effectiveness of the environment.

The result is continuous corporate losses for the stockholders, and eventual bankruptcy where the stakeholders (employees, customers, managers, stockholders, and the surrounding community) lose everything, except for the top management of these companies who retire comfortably to Tahiti with their stock options by selling them in advance. This is an extreme example. However, if this sounds familiar to you, it should, because this was the result of the traditional management philosophy we all saw in the news in 2002, affecting such companies as Enron and WorldCom. This was the result of placing individual agendas over corporate goals. If managers don't care how their employees are treated, can we expect them to care about our customers, corporate profits, or the community?

I wrote this book to contrast the different behavior patterns between traditional management organizations and quality management organizations, and the detrimental effect brought about within an organization by practicing the former. It is important that every manager in a company reads this book and understands traditional management behavior patterns, and how practicing these behaviors over quality management behaviors are detrimental to a company. However, only a Chief Executive Officer (CEO) can take the quality management concepts outlined in this book and make them a reality within the corporation, by requiring all managers, top to bottom, to take these behaviors to heart. In order for a corporation to reap the benefits of using quality management principles, the CEO has to make it a way of life within the organization, and terminate managers that do not practice these behaviors. The CEO also needs to ensure that his or her hard work and success at the corporate reins is not dismantled by a successor who is a traditional CEO.

Many good quality management books have been written over the years, but most have been about how certain companies have achieved success, and not what steps can be taken for every company to achieve success. Quality management can be separated into two aspects: quantitative and qualitative. I will not cover the quantitative (measurements) aspect in this book, because I find that even traditional organizations do those well, because they are a necessity even under that management style. Therefore, I will not be covering such measurement criteria as Six Sigma[4], JIT (Just In Time)[5], or Zero Defects[6] within this book.

The qualitative (how well one treats employees, customers, colleagues, vendors, and other managers) aspect is more important, because this is the foundation of the entire quality management philosophy, and the quantitative aspect will follow as a natural extension of doing business. Each chapter heading is a quality management principle. I will explain its meaning, the skills required to master it, and depict quality management benefits in contrast to the traditional management outcomes by citing real life examples. Even though it is impossible to cite a specific quality management example for every situation encountered in the business world within this book, I think the reader will walk away with an understanding of the behavior pattern to apply to his or her individual circumstances.

The quality commandments outlined in this book will also have a major effect on one's social life as well. We all understand the result of using power and its related behavior patterns at home. This book is meant as a practical guide of quality management's best practices. I have taken existing quality management concepts and expanded on them, using my own experiences, observations, readings, and thought process. This book compares the behavior patterns of quality managers to those of traditional managers, and the end results of each. What makes this book unique from all the other books in the marketplace on business management and leadership is that I discuss traditional management behavior patterns, which up until this point has been considered a taboo to discuss in the world of management. Since traditional employees become traditional managers, this book is meant for everyone in a company, not just management. The objective is to persuade corporations to pursue the quality management philosophy. As you read this book, you will realize that these concepts are common sense, but unfortunately, not to traditional managers.

The examples cited in this book are not meant to reflect poorly on any individual or organization, they are simply meant to depict the differences in style between the traditional management and quality management philosophies. The customer service examples are simply my personal opinion, and are used to illustrate the differences between a bad and a good customer service experience. These examples are not meant to reflect on the business conduct of an entire company. Most companies in the world fall into the gray area, somewhere between traditional management and quality management behavior. My contention is, that if companies in any industry desire to achieve the highest pinnacle of corporate success (measured by continuous growth and profitability), and always maintain that position, the quality management principles outlined in this book have to become a way of life.

I would like to hear from the reader concerning this book and whether or not it was beneficial to you and your organization.

Carpe diem,

Ajit Silva
ajitsilva@rcn.com

Introduction

One concept in quality management philosophy is known as **Employees—Customers—Owners** (ECO), meaning that if your employees are happy, they will go out of their way to provide world-class customer service (exhibited by the employee behaviors outlined in this book that result in profitability). The customers in turn will be very satisfied with a company's product and service, and they will buy additional product and service (customer loyalty) from a company, leading to an increase in company profits, stock price, and market share. E-C-O should be a never-ending process, because you never reach your goal, but keep raising the bar every year.

Ten commandments are mentioned in this book: employee champion, customer champion, continuous improvement, a learning organization, relationship building, empowerment, leadership, paradigm shift, task force, and corporate goals, not individual agendas. No matter the order you prefer to arrange these topics, it was not by mistake that the employee champion chapter was included prior to the customer champion chapter. This is because everything starts and ends with the employee. Prior to addressing quality management behaviors, I want to address traditional management behaviors in the corporate environment. Have you ever experienced any of the following at your workplace?

- Employees have to walk on eggshells because management reacts by shooting first, and asking questions later.

- Employees have to constantly watch their backs, because other employees and managers need someone else to blame for their incompetence.

- Having worked for traditional management organizations all their lives, employees are unable to succeed in a quality management organization, because their empowerment has been stifled over the years.

- Mistakes are not tolerated.

- Customers are given what the company produces, and not what they need.

- Management ignores employee and customer concerns.

- Management takes credit for what their employees have accomplished.

- Management does not practice what it preaches.

- Knowledge is not shared among employees, because it is considered job security and an advantage over others.

- Employees are not allowed to question long-established practices that may rock the boat, though they are detrimental to the company.

- Management is unresponsive to employee needs, and doesn't even know their names.

- Forget incentives, employees are told that they are lucky to be employed!

- The same mistakes are continuously made in the workplace.

- Managers seem to be doing everything to make themselves succeed, while leaving the employees that made them successful behind.

- The best employees are not hired or promoted because management considers them a threat.

- Management believes in micro-managing employees.

- Management never apologizes to employees for mistakes it makes.

- Management does not treat all employees equally and practices seniority and nepotism.

- Management does not allow individual thought, expression, or empowerment.

- Management sets employees up to fail.

- Management is not approachable.

- Management and employees do not believe in internal customers.

- Continuous improvement does not exist in the environment.

- Management is reactive to employee and customer needs, instead of being proactive.

- Management never follows through on promises.

- Witch-hunts are organized when it is necessary to find someone to blame.

- Management gives employees written warnings that are unjustified.

- Employee performance is never addressed until year-end when managers choose a performance rating by rolling the dice.

If you are an employee working in such a company, you need to look for another job. If you are a quality manager working for such a company, you need to look for another opportunity, because you will not succeed in an environment surrounded by traditional managers. If you are a CEO ignoring these issues within your company, you had better start looking for another job as well, because stockholders will not tolerate the negative impacts this behavior will have on corporate profits.

On the other hand, as a CEO you still have the opportunity to bring about much needed change, and will look like a hero to the entire company in doing so, if you take action now. Open up the lines of communication (open-door policy) within the organization at the lowest levels, and eliminate all these managers that are destroying the company. I have found in some instances that the CEO is unaware of the behavior exhibited by the management team or never takes the employee's word over that of management. You need to take a pulse on what is transpiring within your corporation, otherwise, it is equivalent to flushing money down the drain.

I applaud those quality managers that continue to work in these types of organizations, despite being considered threats by their counterparts because of their knowledge, never being promoted, and acting as buffers for their employees in the midst of incredible odds. It is unfortunate that most often those who give the most to an organization go unnoticed, because corporate goals are sacrificed for individual agendas. One can do nothing but seek employment elsewhere. But in these times, with the unemployment rate at five percent or greater nationwide, that is not an encouraging option. Therefore, employees and quality managers spend their time trying to survive, rather than being effective within an organization. The next ten chapters will explain how to change a traditional organization into a quality organization. Notice that all these chapters have reoccurring themes. This is because quality managers exemplify certain behaviors that are consistent across all these commandments.

1

Employee Champion

Employees are the front-line to the customers, and unless companies treat employees correctly, employees in return will not treat customers appropriately, resulting in organizations losing business and profits. But in an era in which employees' no longer stay with companies for their entire lives, companies need to attract and keep the best employees by satisfying their needs. This drives employee loyalty and retention. How do organizations become employee champions? Consider incorporating the following practices:

1. **Hire The Best Candidates**

In contrast to conventional thought, companies do not become employee champions after the hiring process ends, it actually happens before individuals are hired into their positions. A company should hire the most qualified candidate for the position, not only for the benefit of the company, but also for the success of the candidate. Under traditional management philosophy this hardly ever happens. For example, if a director fills a management position, he or she tends to look for management candidates less qualified than they are. There is a threat factor that takes over during interviewing, that completely eliminates rational thought.

How do I know this? I have seen great candidates dropped from consideration, though they interviewed perfectly and had a wealth of experience for the position being filled. The response given by other managers and directors is that they didn't feel comfortable with the candidate. They could not elaborate further. This has happened to me during the interview process. Recruiters have told me on several occasions that the director did not want to hire me, because he or she felt that I would be a threat to their position. I guess these companies would rather settle for mediocrity rather than find the best candidate. Would you practice this behavior if you owned your own business? Interestingly enough, these same companies want the employee to perform to the highest levels after being hired, but obviously do not consider that during the hiring process.

1

By the way, let me put an end to that old stereotype—that candidates have the ability to determine the outcome of the interview process by their actions or inactions. This is only partially true. I find that during an interview process, the fate of the candidate is dependant on the candidate, the recruiter (for external candidates) and the hiring manager, doing everything correctly. If one of them did something incorrectly during the hiring process, the candidate will not land the job, even if this individual was perfect for the position.

For example, the candidate can have an excellent resume, can interview perfectly, and submit a thank you letter at the end, all to no avail. The candidate is left to think that maybe someone was more qualified or interviewed better. I can tell you from personal experience that I am excellent at interviews, and I interview for the sake of interviewing, and to see the expressions and reactions of hiring managers when I discuss quality management.

Other than the threat component mentioned above, at times recruiters have not provided me with all the information. For example, a recruiter years ago did not tell me until after the fact, that Charles Schwab offered a 20 percent bonus for a senior management position. If I had known that, my asking price would have been lower, and I would have most likely landed the position. In another instance a recruiter informed me that I was meeting with a technical recruiter, and in fact, it was the hiring manager. The hiring manager did not introduce himself or talk about the job; therefore, I did not know that he was the decision maker until after the interview. Since I didn't know this fact, I did not talk about my experiences or what I would do in the position, because I was thinking that I was meeting the hiring manager next.

Also, many hiring managers do not know how to interview, and they hardly talk about anything during the interview process. They are silent just to see if they can catch the candidate saying something wrong. A company has to give potential candidates a good impression from the very start, if they want an individual to work for them. An interview is a two-way street; the company is not only interviewing the candidate, but the candidate is also interviewing the company. Unfortunately, most companies do not consider this to be the case.

I have seen hiring managers lose great candidates because they want the management team to come to a consensus. Anyone that has ever been at management meetings realizes that the management team rarely comes to a consensus on anything. At this point the leader must step in and make a decision, instead of letting a perfectly great candidate get away, but this rarely happens.

For all the above reasons, the best way for a candidate to land an opportunity is through contacts. Under the traditional management philosophy, this means that candidates do not have to know anything or do anything; they just need to be a relative or an acquaintance. I would not even hire my sister for an opportunity unless she was qualified, because it would be a bad reflection on me as a manager. I worked with a gentleman years ago that was hired into a management position because his daughter had dated the senior manager at one time. The problem was that his background was in office management, and this was an information technology department, and he didn't know a thing about computers.

This is not meant to be a book on interviewing. I mentioned the interview process because quality organizations don't leave anything to chance. These organizations recruit and hire the best candidates for opportunities, even if the candidates are more qualified than they're soon-to-be colleagues or hiring managers. This is because quality organizations consider company success over individual success. They realize that if one does things right by the company, individual success will be a natural outcome, because those who are hired will make their managers shine. Quality managers, unlike traditional managers, rarely hire individuals who totally think like them, because they realize that new ways of thinking and a variety of skills are good for an organization. This is why some companies will not promote a vice-president to a president's position, because these companies require fresh ideas, and they typically need to hire from the outside to take the company in another direction. Traditional organizations concentrate on hiring candidates who think and behave like them, for control purposes.

Another consideration under a quality organization is that these new hires must be promotable to the next level. This concept is not given much thought in traditional organizations. It is important for quality organizations to fill positions with individuals with extensive experience in a particular field, instead of simply hiring acquaintances. Otherwise, the hiring managers will be placing these employees in roles where they are unable to function, which is an injustice to these employees, because they may have been able to fit perfectly in other opportunities, which they forego. The result will be terminations, and a bad reflection on the hiring managers. Companies should also hire candidates that have the skills to perform in a number of positions within the company. Quality organizations look for Renaissance employees who have the skills and motivation to perform in a variety of positions, enabling the company to be profitable with less headcount in bad economic times.

2. <u>Mentor Your Employees</u>

Traditional managers never make an effort to be a mentor, facilitator, and coach to their employees. A company's most valuable asset, the employee, is left to fend for him or herself after being hired. Even in the horse-breeding world, if you wanted your prized horse to win the Kentucky Derby, wouldn't you provide him or her with the proper training? How many of you have accepted a programming position, but got absolutely no training, beyond manuals thrown your way to read and absorb? How many of you have asked for training, not received it, and yet been held accountable for completing a project? How many of you have spent the first week or so trying to get access to applications that you need to perform your job? The traditional managers' attitude is, since you were hired into this position, you should be able to perform your job. This behavior sets employees up for failure and results in attrition and lost revenue for a company.

Quality managers understand that employee success results in company success and profitability. Even before an employee's start date, the work environment (desk, PC, telephone, network connectivity, application access, writing supplies) has been organized. This is not only to make the employee feel a part of the team and to provide a good impression of the company, but to make them productive from the beginning. Mentors will then be assigned to guide the employee in his or her position. This is often a colleague, a manager, or both. The emphasis is on the success of the employee. A part of each individual team member's job performance is based on what that individual contributed to the team or did to assist his or her fellow employees. Team success is given priority over individual success. Individual success will follow by contributing to the team and the company. This does not occur in traditional organizations. There is no emphasis for colleagues to contribute to the development of the new team member. How many of you after joining teams have found that your colleagues frown upon answering your questions? They almost seemed to say, I have knowledge over you that I am not going to share, because it is job security.

Every employee must be given the opportunity to make a contribution to the team and the company, and this starts by providing the new hire with all the necessary tools, which include mentoring the employee. The number one reason employees leave a department or organization is their immediate supervisor. Therefore, a supervisor's performance appraisal should take into account employee attrition, as this has an effect on company profits. It is more cost-effective to make the effort to address an employee's performance by mentoring, than to train a new employee due to attrition.

Of course, there are times, despite all your efforts, an employee will not succeed in his or her position. In this case, quality organizations will terminate this employee, but only after making an effort to assist the employee. Often traditional organizations will not provide the employee with the tools or support necessary to perform the job successfully. As a result, any inaction on the employee's part will not be tolerated, and the employee will be terminated or placed in another department. This self-fulfilling prophecy (management creates the conditions for an employee to fail, and then blames the employee) will benefit neither the employee nor the organization.

3. **Development Plans and Continuous Performance Appraisals**

The importance of development plans, a process by which management develops each employee's skills and contributions to the organization in order to promote him or her to the next level, cannot be over-emphasized. Traditional organizations do this as an afterthought, or not at all. Quality organizations use this tool to improve the quality and contributions of each employee from the time they are hired and for succession planning—the process by which employees are mentored and trained to take another employee's position because of promotion or attrition.

Quality organizations use the development plan (training and projects the employee has completed to be promoted) in conjunction with their continuous performance appraisal process (how the employee is performing in the present position over a period of a year) during a monthly or quarterly one-on-one (employee-manager meeting) with each employee. This is a meeting in which a manager and an employee discuss the employee's progress (courses taken and contributions made) over a period of time, i.e. quarter, from agreed upon objectives, and what the employee hopes to accomplish in future months. Therefore, if an employee was consistently performing well in a number of objectives, the manager could tell the employee to concentrate on other objectives that have not been met. It is a way to develop an employee's knowledge, performance, and contribution to an organization.

An objective given the employee to accomplish should be realistic and agreed upon by both parties. For example, if the employee is working on a project in addition to regular job functions, a reasonable time for completion should be determined by considering the scope of what needs to be accomplished versus available resources (if the employee needed to get others involved). Also, any objective on the yearly performance appraisal should be measurable. For example, if the employee were a help desk or call center agent, a traditional organization may note on the employee's performance appraisal, that he or she must increase the number of calls taken and lower the time on each customer call.

Quality organizations will note on the employee's performance appraisal that he or she should increase the average daily number of calls answered by twenty calls, and reduce the time spent on each call by thirty seconds to achieve a time of three hundred seconds (five minutes) for each call, to obtain a rating of three. By using a continuous performance appraisal process on a monthly or quarterly basis, quality managers ensure that employee and corporate objectives are met, while being fair to the employee.

Traditional managers are not likely to use continuous performance appraisals or development plans and therefore do not foster continuous improvement within the organization. As a result, employees pay the price at year-end when traditional managers flip coins to determine employee ratings, which effects annual salary increases, bonuses, and promotions. Employees, realizing that there is no fairness or objectivity in determining these ratings by traditional organizations, leave these companies. The unacceptable part that has an affect on a company's bottom line is that the employees who leave these organizations may in fact be excellent employees and not just non-performers.

Quality organizations use development plans and continuous performance appraisals to retain exceptional employees (otherwise, how can a manager differentiate performance?) and to develop exceptional leaders who will one day run the organization.

4. **Treat All Employees Well**

Treating employees well does not cost companies a lot of money, and yet the rewards from this type of corporate behavior in terms of productivity, customer satisfaction, increased morale, loyalty, reduced attrition, and increased revenue and market share, can be tremendous. Quality organizations trust, respect and empower employees; they provide incentives, bonuses and awards, opportunities for advancement; they reward performance, acknowledge good performance immediately in front of colleagues, follow through on promises, and lead by example. Unlike traditional managers, quality managers observe employees doing things right. The culture created makes the employee excited to come to work daily, and the stress level is considerably reduced. Also, happy employees tend to be more productive.

Here are a few companies that practice quality behaviors as listed in Fortune Magazine's 2005 issue concerning "The 100 Best Companies To Work For." The companies got on this list, based two-thirds on what employees had to say about their workplace, and one-third based on company feedback on its people policies, practices, and philosophies. Note that the companies are from a variety of industries and include both large and small corporations. The goal is to stay on this list yearly:

- Wegmans Food Markets (1)

- W.L. Gore (2)

- Republic Bancorp (3)

- Genentech (4)

- Xilinx (5)

- J.M. Smucker (6)

- S.C. Johnson & Son (7)

- Starbucks (11)

- SAS Institute (16)

- Cisco Systems (27)

- American Cast Iron Pipe (28)

- Stew Leonard's (29)

- Amgen (33)

- American Express (37)

- Symantec (43)

- Four Seasons Hotels (51)

- A.G. Edwards (56)

- Microsoft (57)

- General Mills (58)

- Marriott International (63)

- Intuit (64)

- SEI Investments (70)

- Vanguard Group (72)

- Eli Lilly (73)

- CarMax (87)

- Nordstrom (88)

- MBNA (89)

- Harley-Davidson (92)

- Publix Super Markets (94)

- FedEx (96)[7]

Here are several examples of why the companies above are on the list:

Xilinx new hires at this specialty chipmaker receive stock-option grants. It continued its no-layoff policy by requiring management to take a 20 percent pay cut. CEO Wim Roelandts prides himself on responding promptly to employees' e-mail questions.[8]

The success of Stew Leonard's, a family-owned grocery store, is largely due to the company's passionate approach to customer service: Rule No.1:The customer is always right. Rule No. 2: If the customer is ever wrong, re-read rule No.1. This principle is so essential to the foundation of the company that it is etched in a three-ton granite rock at each store's entrance. In order to create happy customers, Stew Leonard's is also recognized for its management philosophy: Take good care of your people and they in turn will take good care of your customers.[9]

Quality managers also right any previous injustices done to an employee by a previous manager. They do not look the other way and say what is done is done. They take personal responsibility to right the wrong. When managers do this, they gain their staff's respect. Remember, respect has to be earned; it is never handed to an authority figure. Traditional managers do none of the things I mention above, and do everything I mentioned in the introduction to this book. They manage by control and fear.

What makes a quality organization is not doing one or two things correctly, or a few managers who practice quality behavior. It is creating a culture where managers and employees know to do the right thing and exhibit correct behaviors at all times. Quality managers do not favor one employee over another, all are treated equally. Also, these organizations institute an open-door policy by which concerns can be brought up to any level of the organization, unlike traditional organizations in which the issue does not go any further than the immediate manager because of a fear of reprisal.

As a result, quality organizations have no need to micro-manage employees and managers, as in traditional organizations. The extra energy can be concentrated on beating the competition, which is the real threat, not an organization's employees. As stated before, the only individual who can bring about this global mindset change within an organization is the CEO.

5. **Create Win-Win Outcomes**

Whenever you deal with anyone—customers, colleagues, managers, employees, strangers, or family, it is important to create a win-win outcome in which both parties walk away from the conversation feeling good about the events that just transpired. You never know when you will require their services in the future, so it is important to build and maintain the relationship. This is especially important if you are looking to change an employee's behavior. You need to be able to correct the behavior without lowering the employee's productivity, and at the same time, maintain the working relationship. Here is an example:

Years ago when I was managing an IBM outsourced help desk for Computer Task Group (CTG), the supervisor came to me and said he was having a problem with an employee who was constantly coming to work late. This employee was covering second shift on weekends (2:30 PM–11:00 PM), and often would show up late or not come in at all. The fear was that the individual that worked on first shift (6:30 AM–3:00 PM) might go home, leaving no one to cover the desk, if this trend continued. The supervisor had already spoken to this individual, to no avail.

Had I been a traditional manager, I would have called the employee into my office and told him that this behavior was unacceptable, and the next time he arrived late at work, he would be fired. But that would have accomplished nothing other than attrition, low morale from the rest of the staff, a time period that I needed to train and fill a new employee, and an unhappy customer. Those who have worked in outsourcing know that these customers scrutinize everything and are very difficult to please.

I spoke with the employee and explained the situation to him in a logical manner. I said that we were under an outsourcing contract and obliged to meet certain service levels. If he did not come in at the required time, and the individual on A-shift went home, it would cause an exposure that would be difficult to explain to the customer, especially since the outsourcing took place at the customer site. As a matter of fact, this sort of thing may even lead to us losing the customer's business, and then all of us would be out of a job.

In the midst of my conversation with the employee, I discovered that he was late constantly because he was having car trouble. He was too embarrassed to mention it, so he was calling in sick or arriving at work late. I told him that I understood, but we needed to rectify the situation immediately, because it was an unacceptable exposure to the customer. I informed him, that he had three options: fix the car, move closer to work (he lived about forty-five minutes away, and moving closer meant that he could even have a roommate drop him at work, when required), or purchase another car.

My employee decided to purchase another car. He was thankful that I had explained the situation to him, and not simply fired him. If I had been a traditional manager, I would never have learned about the car situation, and would not have cared. My employee's performance actually improved as a result of our conversation because he realized that his manager respected and cared about him. Quality managers realize that they have to go that extra mile for the employee, because it makes good business sense. Not only did this encounter result in no attrition, and improved productivity, but also he informed others at the help desk that I was an exceptional manager; therefore, I gained immediate respect from the rest of my staff.

The small things we do often go a long way. Getting along with everyone and creating win-win outcomes will help both employees and managers further their careers up the corporate ladder. Traditional managers may climb the corporate ladder, mostly due to contacts, but will not last long because of their total lack of interpersonal skills and pure self-interest, which will have a major effect on corporate profits, because employees drive revenue. Employees are the workers, and the next time a traditional manager speaks down to an employee, he or she should think about who is helping to further his or her career. Traditional managers do not feel that employees can further their career, only their boss, so they do not spend the time building lasting relationships with employees.

However, I have worked in companies where the employee becomes the manager, and vice-versa. Now the importance of building that relationship is really tested. Whereas, in traditional management relationships, employees are reluctant to do extra work for their managers, quality managers can get employees to perform work for them without requesting, because of the tremendous caring and respect employees have for these managers.

6. **Retain Exceptional Employees**

Did you ever wonder why traditional organizations laid off their best employees, while retaining the unproductive ones? It certainly does not make any business sense, and the message to the staff is that performance does not matter. Unfortunately, layoffs have become inevitable in recent times, because of foreign competition and market conditions. Though layoffs are a necessary evil, traditional organizations view it quit differently than quality organizations. Traditional managers will look at a layoff as a means of eliminating staff without giving any consideration to the performance of the individuals in these positions. As a matter of fact, they may even say, last in—first out (LIFO). They consider this behavior fair to the individuals and to the company, but in reality, it is fair to neither.

A quality manager faced with a layoff situation looks at the performance of the individuals in these positions. To this manager, seniority is not a consideration, but rather each individual's contribution to making the company successful. Remember, in times of layoffs, a company needs to retain not only exceptional performers, but also versatile ones who are willing to perform more than one job function. Therefore, a quality manager reviewing performance will recognize that even though a particular position has to be eliminated, the individual in the position has done x, y, z for the company above and beyond their job expectations. Quality managers, if at all possible, will place these individuals in another department until the layoff subsides, because they realize that others cannot replace these individuals.

The myth under the traditional management system has been that anyone can be replaced. This is false. You cannot replace individuals who are empowered and go above and beyond for a company by doing additional projects that fall outside their job description. These are individuals who love to work (workaholics) for pure satisfaction, and not for monetary gain. They are the exceptional few that add value (because they do the work of two or three people, without requesting compensation in return) to a company, but go unrecognized in traditional organizations because managers care only about saving their own necks (individual agendas). Traditional managers may even lay off these exceptional workers prior to their performance appraisals to justify this behavior in their minds.

I can certainly empathize with this entire scenario. Twice companies have laid me off, despite my being an exceptional worker and doing additional projects, while others who have not made my contribution have been retained. I have had only one employee, in all my years of management, who was an exceptional worker and performed additional projects without being required to. Be assured that I would never lay off such an individual, even if it meant sacrificing my own position, because this type of individual makes one proud to be a quality manager. Traditional organizations are hurting their productivity and profitability by laying off exceptional employees using the LIFO (last in-first out) and seniority criteria, instead of basing it on performance.

7. **Employee Satisfaction Surveys and Focus Groups**

Upper management (director level and above) must take a pulse on what is occurring within their organization. Traditional managers often will act one way but tell their superiors something totally different. Conducting employee satisfaction surveys and convening focus groups at least once a year will rectify that situation and go a long way toward employee loyalty and retention, because employees will conclude that upper management listens and acts upon their concerns.

Organizations who champion employees will practice all these behaviors. To be considered a quality organization, these behaviors have to be practiced consistently by all parties. All this will result in happy employees, and that equates to increased morale, higher productivity, empowerment, and less absenteeism; also, company loyalty, less attrition, increased customer satisfaction, and increased profits, and eventual business expansion. Remember, ECO (employees—customers—owners)—everything starts and ends with how well employees are treated.

2

Customer Champion

In today's world economy, companies cannot be profitable, or for that matter survive, without being a customer champion—providing excellent customer service daily that delights and retains customers. This has become a necessity because we live in a global economy where competition is fierce. We do not always think about this when we go about our daily occupations. We think that companies simply exist to give us jobs to satisfy our survival needs. However, none of us would be employed if not for the customers that continue to purchase products and services that those companies' offer and that make them successful and profitable. This issue becomes clear in times of layoffs. How do companies become customer champions? Consider incorporating the following practices:

1. <u>Develop a Market Niche</u>

Companies cannot compete in all markets and be successful, especially if the company is a start-up or small concern trying to compete with giants in the industry. They cannot be all things to everyone. Companies such as General Electric are exceptions because of the vast amount of resources they command. Whether the company is small or large, in order to be successful and stay successful, it should concentrate on a particular market niche—its field of expertise. For example, Eastman Kodak, a leader in imaging technology, had purchased a company known as Sterling Drug in 1988, but the company was very unprofitable because Kodak did not have expertise in this particular field. Kodak realized this about six years later and sold Sterling Drug in 1994.

Companies should also give themselves time to grow, without competing in every market. Wal-Mart has been number one on the Fortune 500 list of companies for the past four years (2002–2005)[10], even though 20 years ago, it only had stores in about half of the United States, even though it was started in 1962. It was not that Wal-Mart could not afford to expand to every state, but it made more business sense to grow slowly, and gave the firm a competitive edge. Wal-Mart is a big success because it leads the competition in two out of three ways by which companies compete—operational excellence and customer intimacy.[11]

Operational excellence means that Wal-Mart uses the company's infrastructure as a competitive weapon. For example, Wal-Mart has its own satellite system for management meetings; it stocks shelves twice a week, and competitors replenish once in two weeks; it uses cross-docking (the company does not keep inventory and re-orders supplies area-wide for multiple stores at the same time, supplies that are picked up by Wal-Mart trucks at a central location); all the buildings are built to look alike, and the same materials are used for construction. All this brings Wal-Mart considerable savings, which they pass on to consumers in the form of lower prices. It is the same high quality products that are sold at other department stores, thereby increasing Wal-Mart's market share.

Customer Intimacy means that Wal-Mart associates are very courteous, helpful, and knowledgeable when customers seek assistance. Customers usually would not mind paying extra for this type of service.

The third means by which companies compete—product leadership[12] does not fall into Wal-Mart's realm. This method of competition refers to companies such as Intel Corporation, which invent products and continuously strive to beat their own standards. For example, when Intel invented the Pentium III processor, it was most likely inventing the Pentium IV processor in another part of the building to stay one step ahead of the competition and continue to be the market leader.

Another perfect example of a company that dominates its market niche is Wegmans Food Markets, a grocery store chain that I grew up with in Rochester, NY. In 2005, Wegmans was voted No.1 in Fortune Magazine's "The 100 Best Companies To Work For."[13] It is considered one of the premier grocery stores in the U.S. (people come from across the U.S. to see Wegmans), and is a true quality management organization. As a result, I knew that one day Wegmans would achieve this stature.

Visit Wegmans, where you will find the freshest fruit and vegetables, an incredible bakery (baked goods and desserts), a Chinese food section, a sushi section, a child play center (watches kids while you shop), a dry cleaner, a bookstore, a florist, a wine shop, a pharmacy, a photo lab, and a coffee and tea café. Wegmans is not simply a grocery store it is an event. Once customers arrive, they do not feel like leaving. As customers shop, throughout the store Wegmans employees serve the latest dishes that are on sale. You could have yourself a good meal simply by walking around the store.

I have never purchased a bad fruit or vegetable at Wegmans, as their quality control is amazing. Also, I have encountered employees at Wegmans who have worked there since high school, and who continue to work there. It treats its employees extremely well. Wegmans operates in the grocery retail industry and relies heavily on younger workers. Danny Wegman, president of Wegmans Food Markets, Inc. realized some time ago that he needed to do something to retain these younger workers.

Since incorporating a work-scholarship connection program in 1987 which gave students $2,500 a year as college tuition assistance, eighty percent of the program's graduates not only completed high school and went on to higher education, but have stayed with Wegmans, saving the company much money in attrition costs.[14] In 2004, Wegmans Food Markets voluntary attrition rate was 6 percent, great for its industry and for employing 30,128 workers. Almost 6,000 employees (20 percent of the work force) have ten years or more of service, and another 806 employees have greater than 25 years of service.[15] However successful, Wegmans is located in only four states at the present time. This marketing strategy has allowed Wegmans to concentrate on a market region and dominate its market. Due to the company's emphasis on excellent customer service, when Wegmans moves into an area, it usually drives out the competition.

A company will be much more successful and profitable if the company can provide excellent customer service to a hundred percent of its customers in several states, rather than providing mediocre service to customers in all fifty States. It is better to be a big fish in a small pond, rather than a small fish in a big pond.

2. **Listen to Customers and Satisfy Their Needs**

Think back in time to the 1920s. If you walked into a corner grocery store to buy a product, maybe a certain brand of soap, and found that the merchant did not sell it, you had to purchase what was available. If you asked the merchant if he or she could start selling your brand of soap, the answer you would have received was no, because it was not a consumer or market-driven economy at the time, but rather a merchant-driven economy. He or she would have told you to buy their product or go elsewhere. You could not have gone elsewhere because the next closest store may have been twenty miles away, and not everyone had a car at the time. Therefore, consumers were forced to buy what merchants sold. Think about what happens today if you walk into a store and it does not sell a brand of soap that you want. You simply drive or walk on over to Wal-Mart, which sells many brands of soap and many different types of consumer products. As a result, competition has gotten much more fierce and merchants have to do everything possible to retain customers. These days we live in a world economy and a customer-driven, service-oriented market. For example, products assembled in the United States may have parts arriving from around the world; therefore, boundaries no longer matter, as seen by the Internet. In order to be competitive and profitable in today's market place, satisfying customer needs is more important than simply selling products.

How do companies know what their customers' needs are? Why not simply ask? Companies can accomplish this in a variety of ways such as customer satisfaction surveys, suggestion boxes, and telemarketing calls. However, the best method at a company's disposal is through focus groups. Monthly focus groups should be held with a panel of eight to twelve customers to determine satisfaction levels with service as well as to obtain suggestions for marketing new products or improvements. As an example, years ago Stew Leonard's, the quality supermarket chain previously mentioned, was having problems selling its strawberries in sealed containers. When a panel of customers was asked about this issue, the management was informed that customers do not like to purchase strawberries in cartons because the ones at the bottom are always damaged. The customers preferred the strawberries out in the open so they could pick and choose their own. Whether there was an issue with the strawberries being in cartons or not, companies have to cater to customer perceptions. The customers also informed the grocery store management that when they purchase strawberries for one or two people, they are not looking to buy a lot, so they would like the strawberries sold by the half pound, instead of by the pound. When the management implemented these changes, sales went up by fifty percent. This solution may not work in every grocery store or every region, but the point is that the management listened to its customers, and satisfied their needs by using focus groups. Whenever companies can contact their customers and convene focus groups, prior to selling a product, the product will have a better chance of selling.

In 1992 this customer service philosophy allowed Stew Leonard's to be inducted into the Guinness Book of World Records for having the greatest sales per square foot of any single food store in the United States. Stew grossed over $85 million in one location just selling a handful of items such as chicken, cheese, eggs, and muffins. The average grocery store sells a bit over $300 per square foot, whereas Stew Leonard's cashes in around $3,000 a square foot by making it a pleasure to shop in his store. He has a petting zoo for kids, a mechanical chicken that lays eggs, and a wall that depicts thousands of customers prominently displaying Stew Leonard's shopping bags.[16]

Traditional organizations do not tend to ask customers about their products prior to selling them, or for that matter prior to making them. Customers either buy what they have or go elsewhere. This philosophy worked fine in the early Nineteenth Century when multiple department stores did not exist on every block, when there was no foreign competition, and there was no Internet. It will hardly work these days. This is why Sears got out of the catalog mail order business, as there are many more ways for customers to buy products in the modern world.

Most of the companies in the U.S. still follow this traditional management philosophy to an extent. In the U.S. for example, the automobile industry designs cars, develops, markets, and sells them. Then they find out that a particular car may not even sell. By contrast, the Japanese auto industry performs market research by asking a number of their customers prior to the automobile being developed if the marketplace would be willing to purchase such an automobile if it were made. If this test sample said yes, the car would be developed; otherwise, it would be scratched. As a result, the Japanese auto industry saves a lot of otherwise wasted money on research and development, marketing, and sales. In the future, more automobiles will be made to customer specifications instead of being purchased in a showroom.

3. **Actively Resolve Customer Issues**

Anyone who has contacted a call center or help desk has experienced the frustration of having to call back multiple times in order to get a problem resolved. Quality organizations make every attempt to resolve customer problems on the first call, otherwise known as first call resolution. This is a customer satisfaction index at call centers and help desks. To achieve this objective, these organizations may provide their agents with additional training, keep documentation current, or resolve system and network problems expeditiously—anything to answer customer inquiries or resolve problems promptly.

Quality organizations will also take these measures one-step further and resolve problems or prevent problems from occurring in the first place. If the information technology organization of a wireless service provider, for example, knew that a network device was reaching the end of its life, why not have a regularly scheduled maintenance program to replace any such device, prior to it causing a problem and interrupting service to customers? Also, a wireless provider does not need to hear from customers in certain parts of the country stating that they have no service. The company already knows this fact because they know where their cell towers are located and whether or not they have roaming agreements with other carriers. If this lack of service in certain regions is known in advance, cell phones should not be sold to these customers. In this case, customers should be told that they would receive better service from a competitor, but that in the future this company will have service in that region.

Customers prefer honesty to trying to sell a product that does not work. This goodwill will pay dividends in the future, as the company will gain a reputation for integrity and excellent customer service. These customers may in fact return some day, whereas if the customers are lied to, the business will lose them forever. Wireless service providers that sell customers cellular phones and rate plans where there is no coverage do not realize that they are hurting their own branding. The whole idea is to have lifetime customers. There are also indirect marketers for wireless service providers that will market cell phones in regions where the company has no coverage, just to make a quick commission.

The wireless companies have less control over these stores than their own, because the product has already been purchased and is being resold. However, these carriers should keep track of customer complaints from both within their stores and also relative to indirect marketers. Damage to a company's reputation (branding) will result in a considerable loss of market share and future profit potential.

Quality organizations resolve problems actively to eliminate a considerable cost to the company and improve the company's bottom line. If customers have to call back multiple times in order to resolve their issues, that means that a company is spending much more money staffing a call center or help desk than is necessary. These companies get to the reason of these reoccurring calls and resolve them once and for all. Root cause analysis will be discussed in detail in the next chapter. Another important reason organizations need to resolve problems actively is the potential loss of existing business and future business. Customers complain a minimum of seven times to acquaintances when they are dissatisfied with a company's service, but only tell one or two people when they are satisfied with the service. Since companies cannot measure this potential loss of business, it is a competitive advantage to resolve problems immediately, and ensure that they do not reoccur.

4. <u>Project A World-Class Attitude</u>

I am amazed in this day and age how many organizations still do not practice the policy that the customer is always right. I have worked for organizations in which employees interrogate and speak very rudely to customers, and the management does nothing to put an end to this type of behavior. We all understand that customers are not always right, and some may even try and take advantage of organizations by complaining for no reason to receive free services or products. However, the customer is always right philosophy is a mindset that has to be embraced and exercised by organizations. If employees do not practice this principle, all the customers who have legitimate reasons for complaining will be ignored, which is exactly what happens in organizations. Since employees are often unable to separate legitimate complaints from fantasies, this principle must be adhered to at all times in order to provide excellent customer service and to retain customers. Otherwise, these customers will take their business elsewhere, resulting in lost profits and market share.

I have found that most customer complaints are legitimate, and those that try to take advantage of an organization are a very small percentage. This is because most consumers have very busy lives and do not have time to plan to take advantage of organizations. A majority of the complaints by customers in regard to company products (other than clearly defective products issues) may have to do with companies not educating consumers on what they purchased. For example, if a wireless service provider sold a rate plan to a customer, some of the things that should be explained to the customer are: Whether the plan is a regional or nationwide plan, how many minutes come standard with the plan, how much additional it costs per minute if the customer used up the monthly minute allotment, whether nights or weekends are included in the plan or if they cost extra, and the areas where the customer will not receive good reception. If all this is not clearly explained to customers, of course they will call and complain when the monthly bill is received and they see discrepancies; would you not do the same thing? A perfect example is the regulatory deductions and taxes charged on a local phone bill. How many of us truly understand those deductions on our billing statements? Even after speaking with local telephone company representatives, I still do not understand some line items. Also, local phone companies do not go out of their way to make the bills clear either, thereby avoiding a tremendous number of phone calls to their call center. This is known as resolving problems to reduce costs within an organization (because companies need additional staff if customers call back five times when their issue can be resolved on the first call, or prior to calling), which unfortunately most organizations do not tend to understand.

Quality organizations continuously emphasize this world-class attitude through behavior modification controlled by quality assurance departments that monitor customer calls. These organizations expect the best from their employees—to be courteous, friendly, and knowledgeable towards customers, and also to do the right thing, thereby ensuring continued patronage. These organizations understand that the total customer experience matters.

Since many products are purchased and serviced over the phone, an employee's tone in dealing with customers has taken on paramount importance. No customer wants to wait on hold for two minutes or more and speak to a representative who does not sound friendly, courteous, and knowledgeable, or care about resolving their problem. Quality organizations that do all the above correctly and continuously practice world-class customer service, will greatly improve their bottom line. As an example, Nordstrom's Department Stores have been known to accept customer returns of tires, when they do not even sell tires. At one time, a Federal Express driver who came to pick up your packages had the ability to negotiate prices. Companies act in this manner to maintain customer loyalty and to get a leg up on the competition.
17

In contrast, several years ago, I opened a checking account with Sovereign Bank in downtown Philadelphia. It took them a month to send me my checks, and two months to send my wife's debit card. The bank was downstairs in my office building, and I was speaking to the bank management practically every other day. They were giving me lip service by saying that the checks were in the mail as well as the form my wife had to sign in order to receive the debit card. Every time I went into the bank to inquire on the status of the items in question, the management acted as if I were bothering them. When the bank set up our debit cards, they set it up so we could withdraw from checking only at an ATM, and not from savings. In addition, the bank put a hold on most of my salary direct deposit because I had moved from another state, and was charging me for checks that bounced when I had money in my account. The actions did not make us feel welcome for bringing our business to the bank, and did not make it easy for us to pay our bills, having just moved from another state and having incurred moving expenses. This particular branch also did not convey a sense of urgency in dealing with customers, which quality organizations typically do.

During this same time period, I ordered my wife a cellular phone by calling Cingular Wireless. The individual I was dealing with took three weeks to provide us with a cell phone, when it should have been a one-day activity. I had to keep calling back because I would get disconnected when I was on the line with this individual, and he would not return my call. Sometimes I was on hold for ten minutes prior to getting through. This representative told me that he would fax me the contract papers, but he would not follow through. Unfortunately, because I could not spend time at work dealing with this issue, I had to call once I arrived home, and it seemed as if this particular individual was the only one that worked nights. This was all a very frustrating experience for me, and complaining to Cingular's management did not resolve anything, as I never received a return phone call. The only reason I tolerated this behavior was because the company had a good rate plan and good coverage in the area, and my wife required a cell phone to use for emergencies and weekends. Shortly thereafter, we discovered that her cell phone for whatever reason did not work most of the time, and so we ended up dropping the service, but not before paying about six months of service fees on the contract.

Customers should never have to deal with this type of frustration as a result of employee incompetence or company red tape. World-class organizations put the customer first, have a sense of urgency, care about not inconveniencing the customer, and understand the result of their inactions to the company's bottom line. The bank and wireless service provider I mentioned have some customer service issues to resolve because they did not project a world-class attitude, and as a result, lost our business.

5. **Provide Added Value**

Whether your organization competes on the basis of being the lowest cost provider (Wal-Mart), innovations (Sony), differentiating itself from the competition (Dell), or providing excellent customer service (Walt Disney Corporation), none of this matters unless your product or service creates added value to the consumer through quality workmanship or mentality. For example, in the outsourcing industry, added value is created by satisfying more than contractual agreements. Otherwise, why would customers choose an IBM Global Services over a competitor such as Spherion Corporation? It is not always the experience in a particular industry that customers look for, although that certainly does help. Customers look for added value in the form of freebees that companies include. In this particular industry, that may include such things as performing projects to make the environment more effective and efficient, or having a sound problem management and change management process to stop reoccurring problems in the environment. These are in addition to the daily activities such as meeting service level agreements, which are contractually obligated. Are customers willing to pay more for this type of service? Yes, as customers do not mind paying extra for a quality product or service.

In the Automobile Industry for example, consumers are willing to pay more for a BMW over a Volkswagen. Why? Well, consider the higher quality materials used to construct the BMW, consider the engineering, consider the craftsmanship, consider the longevity, consider the fact that the BMW has fewer defects, consider the innovation, and consider the resale value. If you are a consumer who is simply looking to get from one destination to another, then the Volkswagen will satisfy your needs. However, if you are looking for a driving experience, then you will choose the BMW and gladly pay more. The BMW also signifies a certain status, but if the car were not exceptional in performance and reliability, consumers would not purchase it.

In the PC Industry, Dell Computers provides a quality product by having fewer defects than the competition, customization for the consumer, home delivery, and excellent customer service. This added value mentality has given Dell Computers a loyal customer base and allowed it to become the number one selling computer in the world. With the price of technology continuing to decrease, and Dell PCs coming down in price, the company is finding a whole new market of consumers. In 1984, the year Dell started selling PCs, Commodore and IBM had 27 percent and 20.1 percent market shares, respectively. In 2004, Dell Computers had a 33.1 percent share of the PC market, Commodore was no longer in existence, IBM has exited the PC business by selling out to Chinese firm Lenovo, and Hewlett-Packard only has 19.5 percent of the market, despite its merger with Compaq a number of years ago. Dell Computers revenue per employee has risen from $745,000 in 1998 to $900,000 in 2005. Dell's business model has managed to conquer cost, quality, and service, while staying away from building proprietary systems, as was the case when IBM developed OS/2. This has allowed Dell to be profitable and take market share away from the competition in an industry with low profit margins. Due to the many reasons mentioned above, and the fact that at the present time one out of three computers sold in the U.S. is a Dell, Dell Computers was voted the No. 1 company in Fortune Magazine's 2005 list of "America's Most Admired Companies."[18]

I was used to taking my car to Jiffy Lube because there was always one close to where I resided. They provided good service, but did not inform me what they were checking with respect to my car, and they made me wait about one hour on average whenever I took my car in for an oil change. Several years ago, I moved from the Philadelphia area to the Allentown, PA, area, and did not have a Jiffy Lube close to my residence. However, down my street, I found a Valvoline oil change service center. I had not even heard of Valvoline previously, and did not know what kind of service to expect, but was pleasantly surprised. I drove into the service center about ten minutes prior to closing, so I did not expect them to even service my car on that particular day. They not only took my car in, but they had me going on my way within ten minutes. The entire time the service personnel were talking to me and informing me exactly what they were doing. Additionally, the cost was comparable to Jiffy Lube. I was so satisfied with the service, that I have been telling all my acquaintances and friends. One of the things usually forgotten in the service industry is customer experience. Valvoline as a corporation has a good understanding of this concept. You can be assured that I will always look up a Valvoline service center to take my car to, no matter where I move.

In the domestic airline industry, the clear winner has been and continues to be Southwest Airlines. In 2003, Southwest earned $442 million in profits, more than all the other U.S. airlines combined. In fact, from 1994 to 2003, Southwest's profits, around 3.6 billion dollars, beat the rest of the industry combined. So how does Southwest continue to defy the odds through top management changes, through the effects of 9/11, and in a very competitive industry, while some competitors are losing billions? Southwest's formula is to offer much lower fares than its competition; fly city to city instead of the hub and spoke model used by other airlines (which considerably cuts down on mileage, and gas costs, and gets customers to their locations faster); They fly only Boeing 737s (one type of plane to maintain); serve no meals, just snacks; they charge no fees to change same fare tickets; they have no assigned seats; and do not have any electronic entertainment.

This formula allowed Southwest to not only beat the competition, but to be the best performing stock in the U.S. from 1972 to 2003, with an incredible 26 percent increase yearly.[19] This proves that a company can be very successful even through bad economic times, if customers are given added value (arrive at destinations faster for a lower cost). In order for Southwest's competitors to catch up, they would need to undergo a paradigm shift (Chapter 8).

Traditional companies seldom care about customer convenience or added value that is created through excellent customer service, quality products, and free offerings for consumer purchases. These companies will always think about charging the customer for every extra item sold, and have no understanding of the loyalty or goodwill that comes from promoting a quality mentality.

6. **Create Convenience Through Automation**

We live in a world where time is money, and we barely have enough hours in the day to get everything done. Keeping this in mind, companies should automate the shopping and service experience for customers as much as possible because convenience is a necessity in today's world. Customers should be able to order their products through the Internet by going to a particular company's home page. They should also be able to submit a service request through that same web page if they encounter a defect with a product. Corporate service departments should be monitoring customer service requests and responding in a timely manner. No longer should a customer have to wait on hold for five minutes to purchase a product or get an issue addressed. Companies should be including online knowledge bases with virtual reps[20] to assist customers in selecting products and resolving problems, along with such elements as online chat, email, and IVR (interactive voice response units) with speech recognition. This is the difference between being considered a good company and being considered world-class.

The technology will initially cost companies much more money, but the return on investment (ROI) will be realized within six months to a year. Here is the best part: It is to a company's advantage to set up web-based systems rather than have help desk or call center agents take customer calls. The reason is that on average an agent answering a phone costs a company help desk, for example between 15 and 25 dollars per call (cost per call = variable costs + fixed costs/number of calls answered), whereas, if a web-based system were set up, each interaction would cost the company between ten and twenty cents. This type of interaction is beneficial to both companies and consumers—a true win-win outcome. However, companies will need to train its consumers to use the web instead of calling by pointing out the benefits such as increased productivity, because the answer will be found faster. The next step in reducing costs would be through outsourcing. Companies have been reducing their help desk and call center costs by forty to fifty percent by outsourcing their non-core business to places such as Mexico and India where there are highly educated and technical individuals to answer calls at a fraction of the cost to the dollar. However, another important cost reducer for companies is to become effective and efficient at what they do, and that is where technology comes into the picture. Therefore, companies should really be taking advantage of both opportunities to reduce their expenses, while at the same time delighting customers through automated convenience. The savings achieved can be passed on to the consumer as well as to the bottom line.

7. **Believe in Internal Customers**

Ask most corporate employees the definition of a customer, and they will give you answers that do not reflect the fact that customers are also internal. This is typically another area that traditional corporations ignore, as evidenced daily by the terrible manner in which employees within internal departments address one another. In many companies, interpersonal skills seem to be reserved strictly for external customers. Management within traditional companies do not comprehend that employees have much more of an effect on one another's behavior and attitude towards their work environment, than the managers themselves do. Every employee in a company deserves to have a pleasant work environment. Employees should be happy to come to work, otherwise, why bother? Employees are productive only when they are happy. Employees with attitude problems can destroy a happy and productive work environment.

Years ago when I worked at an IBM help desk, one female employee had a terrible attitude. She had no respect for her fellow employees and constantly argued with them and called them names. It was neither a professional work environment nor a happy one. Management never addressed this issue and allowed it to continue and climax. The result was that this one employee created about eighty percent turnover at the help desk. If management overlooked employee concerns, it could have at least shown some concern for the company's bottom line. Quality organizations do not tolerate such behavior because they know that such employees are productivity destroyers. Remember the adage, one bad apple can destroy the whole bunch. Not only that, but if employees are treated badly by other employees in their work environment, and management ignores it, these employees may actually take things out on customers out of frustration, or worse, walk in with a machine gun and start taking lives.

In the example above, the employees mentioned were colleagues, not customers. There is another scenario that happens more frequently, and can have more of an effect on customers. This is when employees from one department call another department for assistance on customer concerns. Whenever I have managed employees, I have informed them that there is such a thing as internal customers. I have told them to keep one simple rule in mind when it comes to internal customers: If you call another department, it does not matter who answers the phone—a peer, subordinate, or manager, you are their customer, and they have to service you accordingly. If someone internally calls our department, again, it does not matter who answers the phone, that individual is our customer, and should be treated accordingly.

This is so important because internal departments have to rely on each other to be productive and to respond in a timely manner to customer requests. We all service the same customers in one way or another and affect the company's bottom line through our actions and inactions. This is why whenever someone leaves me a phone call, or sends an e-mail, my response is practically instantaneous, because I believe in the above truth. I have dealt with numerous individuals, both colleagues and members of supporting departments that have taken days to respond to an inquiry. Obviously, these individuals have the impression that I come to work daily to work for myself, and not for customers.

Some years back, I reported to a director at CDI Corporation who never returned phone calls, or responded to e-mails. Traditional companies seem to hire these types of individuals and do not understand the effect they have on a company's bottom line. This individual was really affecting my productivity to the extent that I was happy to be laid off. The next time you have to respond to somebody, please remember the Golden Rule: Do unto others, as you would have them do unto you. I typically receive a timely response from colleagues and other departments who see me responding to their requests quickly. Quality organizations make a practice of emphasizing to their employees that customers are both external and internal. This belief in internal customers will allow your organization to address external customer concerns more rapidly, thereby increasing customer satisfaction and loyalty. At the same time, it will allow an organization to decrease its employee turnover rate, while increasing employee productivity.

Being a champion of customers has to be practiced every moment, not just when employees feel like it. Management should set the standard and monitor for compliance; otherwise, the competition will be more than willing to do so.

3

Continuous Improvement

Continuous improvement should be second nature to everyone in an organization, and is a necessity to stay ahead of the competition and for an organization to maintain its profitability. The days when employees constantly complained about getting extra assignments from the boss and acquiring new responsibilities and skills, should be gone. If your company has employees with this type of attitude, or those who drop everything when their shift ends, then management has not done a very good job during the hiring process. Interestingly enough, the type of employee mentioned above does not see any correlation between their attitude and inaction and their lack of success within the organization, and the organization's profitability. In fact, there is a direct correlation, because employees are the experts at performing their jobs, therefore, are best able to identify and resolve issues. This is bringing decision making down to the lowest levels and empowering employees to be accountable for their work and take pride in working for their organization. Empowerment is a quality management concept that is discussed further in Chapter 6, but is mentioned here to note the fact that each employee can affect his or her organization's success, as long as he or she has the motivation and empowerment for continuous improvement.

Continuous Improvement is only a qualitative concept in the sense that both employees and managers must have the right attitude (not be complacent) to make necessary changes within the organization. In reality, it is a quantitative concept that needs to be backed by real action within the organization. Simply agreeing that it is needed adds no value to an organization. Both traditional managers and quality managers are in agreement that continuous improvement is a necessity within an organization. The only reason for mentioning this concept, when I stated earlier that this book encompassed only the qualitative aspects of a quality organization, is that one cannot speak about quality without adding the concept of continuous improvement and what to do to achieve it.

The difference between quality managers and traditional managers is that quality managers will take action to ensure that continuous improvement occurs, whereas traditional managers will not. As an example, being a quality manager, I believe that a manager cannot improve an environment by keeping things status quo (managing employees and performing the regular management duties required within a position), but rather, one has to do additional work in the form of projects for continuous improvement to take shape. I cannot tell you the number of managers who think that I am crazy every time I mention this concept. In this case, these same managers have the attitude exemplified by the traditional employees above.

Therefore, there should be better controls in the hiring process, when hiring managers as well. Certainly, it makes no sense to promote an employee to a management position who is unwilling to do extra work for the benefit of the department and organization. Let me address what work means in the form of continuous improvement. A manager can work twelve hours a day, but if he or she is not accomplishing any measurable results, it is a waste of time. Therefore, from a quality management perspective, working smart (measured by accomplishments), means much more than working hard (longer hours). Traditional managers will put in long hours, but at the end of the day, what has been accomplished? Simply performing one's job these days is not satisfactory to beat the competition, because the competition may not have this same attitude. For example, in a small startup, numerous individuals may perform multiple jobs due to the lack of funds and because of the need to be successful and survive. This same motivation is not present among employees who work for major corporations, mainly because they do not see the need for this ownership factor. However, in bad economic times, this will become a reality for employees working for major corporations, and a company's hiring process will really be put to the test. IBM Global Services, a company I worked for years ago, provided incentive for their employees to perform at a higher level by declaring that even if a particular employee were the best ever in a certain position, this individual would still be given a low rating during performance appraisal time unless the person worked on projects to continuously improve the work environment. Several years later, this company stated that employees receiving the lowest rating would be terminated. The company had reduced its four-tier rating system to three tiers. This method, successfully allowed the company to eliminate many employees that were considered dead wood, who had come over from an Eastman Kodak merger several years earlier.

How does a corporation instill continuous improvement within its ranks? Understand the four elements that make up any department, and expand this company-wide:

1. **People**

People can be separated into employees and customers. In relation to employees, hire the best fit and most qualified candidates for each position. Do not ever settle until you find the right candidate, and do not hire relatives or acquaintances unless they have proved themselves worthy. Promoting from within is a great idea, but hire from the outside, if suitable candidates are not present within the organization. During the interview process, ask questions that seek out motivated and qualified employees. Once they are hired, empower these employees, and provide management support for needed change. When employees make mistakes, do not blame them as in traditional organizations, as this is very destructive to an organization and can lead to low morale and attrition. Ninety percent of the mistakes that occur in corporations are a result of processes not being corrected by management, and have nothing to do with employees. Practice being an employee champion—bring out the full potential of each employee by treating him or her appropriately as mentioned in Chapter 1. Challenge your company's employees with additional projects and listen to what they have to say, because they are the experts in their particular positions.

In addition, a company should be asking the following questions in relation to customers, and practice being a Customer Champion as mentioned in Chapter 2:

- Do we have a customer satisfaction survey? If not, one needs to be implemented.

- Are we meeting customer SLOs (service level objectives)? For example, at a help desk or call center, the agents have to answer the calls in thirty seconds or less for a ninety percent SLO monthly. If this is not being met, why not? How can the situation be rectified?

- Do the SLOs make sense? In other words, you want to ensure that SLOs do not contradict each other or send conflicting messages to agents. For example, if you set an SLO for each agent to answer sixty customer calls a day, that may interfere with your first call resolution (FCR) objective of eighty percent that ensures that the agent resolves a customer's call on the first attempt, without the customer having to call back. If customers have to call back, that costs a company additional money in terms of staffing requirements.

- Are we providing added value to the customer? For example, if a customer phones a call center asking about cellular minute usage for the month, agents, in addition to providing the customer with this information, should be informing customers that they can obtain this information also through the company website or an option off the interactive voice response unit (IVR), also known as the 1-800 line. In this particular case, the value is in educating the customer. This is actually value for both parties. It will make it easier for the customer to obtain minute usage information, and also eliminate calls to the call center. Another form of added value offered by wireless providers is through promotions (discounts on cell phone purchases) or bonus minutes for being a long-term customer.

- Are we being responsive to customer needs? Using a wireless provider example again, is the company providing customers with the types of rate plans or coverage that they desire? If not, customers will go elsewhere.

- Are we resolving problems? Customers should not have to concern themselves with a company's lack of service (i.e. due to staffing or process issues). When customers purchase a product from a company, they are actually purchasing quality in their mind, because when something goes wrong, the company's reputation is at stake. Therefore, customer satisfaction can be achieved only by resolving issues immediately, otherwise, customers will take their business elsewhere. In the example above, customers may tolerate having bad coverage in their area one day a month (possibly due to a cell tower being down), but not every day. I find that customers tend to want the same outstanding service (hundred percent reliability) that is provided by landlines, (home telephone service) for their cellular phones as well.

2. **Processes**

Processes, the number-one element that affects the productivity and efficiency of a department or organization, run a department and a company. They separate the great companies from the mediocre ones. Processes are needed to identify and correct underlying problems that continue to reoccur in a company, and should be evaluated on an ongoing basis. Below are three process changes that can be instituted to achieve effectiveness and efficiency within an organization:

Process Owners—Whether your company is dealing with problem management, change management, asset management, accounting procedures, human resource procedures, etc., there should be a process owner who is responsible for process and procedure flow, keeping documentation current, and ensuring that other departments understand and adhere to a process. This individual is also the final authority when it comes to resolving departmental conflicts, and making support groups accountable for their actions or inactions. Most of the examples above are from the information technology (IT) arena, but the point here is that process owners must be in charge of major processes in any functional department within the organization, otherwise customer satisfaction, both internal and external, will be sacrificed. As an example, in information technology, the help desk manager is typically the process owner for problem management.

Identify all the processes that are required within a company. A good method in information technology is ITIL[21] (information technology information library), which covers the management systems above as well as continuity management (disaster recovery), financial management and others. Determine whether these processes are being used, and whether they are being used appropriately. The process owners will need to close any gaps that exist in the environment relative to their process (gap analysis—the state of processes today versus where your organization wants to be, and what will be done to reach the desired state).

Root Cause Analysis—This process can eliminate many problems from reoccurring within an environment. Root cause analysis means that an organization needs to learn why certain problems reoccur and to eliminate those issues. Otherwise, customers will go elsewhere. For example, if a customer calls a help desk and an agent addresses a customer issue, that issue should be resolved permanently. The customer should not have to call back several days later with the same issue. Also, when an issue is resolved, it should be resolved for all customers experiencing the problem. Customers should not have to contact the help desk on an individual basis. Resolving problems permanently increases productivity within departments while increasing customer satisfaction and retention. A typical root cause analysis form used within the problem management arena (information technology help desk) may look like the form found on the next page.

Root Cause Analysis Form

Ticket Created By: _____   **Date Created:** __/__/__

Customer's Name: _____(Last, First)

Ticket#: _____

Severity (1–4): ___

Brief Explanation Of Customer's Problem:

_____
_____
_____
_____

Outage Time: (HH:MM)   **Resolved Time: (HH:MM)**
Fixed Time: (HH:MM)   **Ticket Closed Time: (HH:MM)**
Total Outage Time: (HH:MM)

Cause of Failure:

_____
_____

Failing Device: _____

**Root Cause (check one or more): Process/Procedure__ Hardware__
Software__ Network__ Training__**

Resolution/Actions:

_____
_____
_____
_____
_____
_____
_____
_____

Resolution (Ticket Closing Category):

1) _____New Process or Procedure was Created
   Date Created:__/__/__   Name:_____
                       Location:_____

2) _____Reiterated existing Process or Procedure
                       Name:_____
                       Location:_____

3) _____Hardware Fix

4) _____Software Fix

5) _____Network Fix

6) _____Training Fix

The fields within the form on the preceding page can be programmed into a problem management tool such as Remedy, and then extracted in such a manner for reporting purposes. A typical root cause analysis process would look similar to that found on the next page. This is an information technology-based example of root cause analysis, but this type of logic can be applied to any department. A proper root cause analysis process will inform you if a problem that a support group stated was resolved, actually reoccurred. Also, the help desk manager in this case can create a report for a support department that depicts, for example, how many calls and tickets have been generated by not fixing a reoccurring server problem.

A dollar value can be derived from employees being unproductive, thereby forcing the support department to replace the server. For example, if a thousand employees are on a server, and on average each earns 20 dollars an hour, when a server is down for even half an hour, the cost to a company is 10 thousand dollars. If this happens five times a month, the cost is 50 thousand dollars. In this case, a root cause analysis process can be used to justify replacing the server, because in the long run it is more cost effective. Without a proper root cause analysis process, the fact that this defective server was costing a company so much money may never have been detected. The cost above is for internal customers. The cost of a continuously crashing server that is used by external customers is even worse, because these customers will take their business elsewhere. A root cause analysis process exists to prevent such reoccurrences. As noted in the flow-chart, processes can invoke other processes. In this case, the change management process is invoked at a certain point within the root cause analysis flow. The ROI (return on investment) of implementing a root cause analysis process will more than pay for its cost within six months, if not sooner.

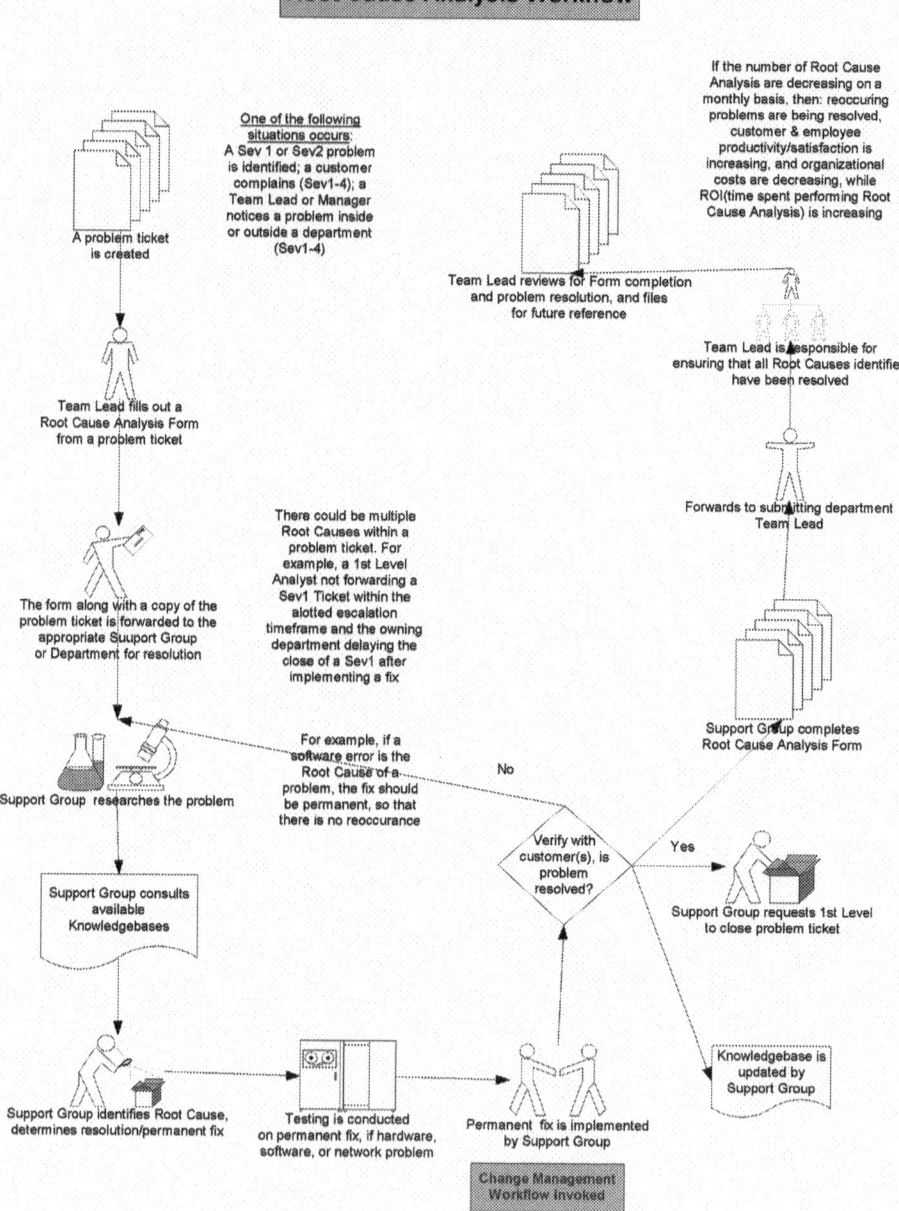

Root Cause Analysis Workflow

A problem ticket is created

One of the following situations occurs:
A Sev 1 or Sev2 problem is identified; a customer complains (Sev1-4); a Team Lead or Manager notices a problem inside or outside a department (Sev1-4)

If the number of Root Cause Analysis are decreasing on a monthly basis, then: reoccuring problems are being resolved, customer & employee productivity/satisfaction is increasing, and organizational costs are decreasing, while ROI(time spent performing Root Cause Analysis) is increasing

Team Lead reviews for Form completion and problem resolution, and files for future reference

Team Lead is responsible for ensuring that all Root Causes identified have been resolved

Team Lead fills out a Root Cause Analysis Form from a problem ticket

There could be multiple Root Causes within a problem ticket. For example, a 1st Level Analyst not forwarding a Sev1 Ticket within the alotted escalation timeframe and the owning department delaying the close of a Sev1 after implementing a fix

Forwards to submitting department Team Lead

The form along with a copy of the problem ticket is forwarded to the appropriate Suuport Group or Department for resolution

For example, if a software error is the Root Cause of a problem, the fix should be permanent, so that there is no reoccurance

No

Support Group completes Root Cause Analysis Form

Support Group researches the problem

Verify with customer(s), is problem resolved?

Yes

Support Group requests 1st Level to close problem ticket

Support Group consults available Knowledgebases

Support Group identifies Root Cause, determines resolution/permanent fix

Testing is conducted on permanent fix, if hardware, software, or network problem

Permanent fix is implemented by Support Group

Knowledgebase is updated by Support Group

Change Management Workflow Invoked

Inhibitor Analysis—Whereas the root cause analysis process can be considered the back-end process for problem resolution (because a problem is addressed reactively), the inhibitor analysis process can be considered the front-end process for problem resolution, because the idea is to prevent problems from occurring in the first place. Let's take an information technology help desk as an example again. If an agent answers a call, and no proper documentation exists to service a customer, that is an inhibitor. If the agent figures out the answer, that person will write it down and may not share it with other team members. A month from now, when another customer calls with the same issue, and another agent answers the call, that person will not know how to handle the situation.

In another scenario, if an agent answers a call for a password reset, and has to assign a ticket to a support group to reset a customer's password, which may take an hour or more (unless an automated system existed that the customer, could use) this is another inhibitor. If the agent had the ability to reset the password, it could most likely be done in about fifteen seconds, and would be a much more productive scenario, not to mention the customer satisfaction that results from resetting it immediately. In the above scenario, sometimes the security department may not give up this right to the help desk because it has always been in charge of password resets. This is a traditional organization mindset that needs to be abandoned for the productivity of the entire organization.

Typically, in these types of situations, agents may inform a manager directly or by e-mail. But managers are very busy and may tend to lose track of the information prior to taking any action. The employee feels that his or her request was neglected, when this was not the case. An inhibitor analysis process exists to rectify these types of situations so an environment can be more productive, thereby increasing employee and customer satisfaction.

A typical inhibitor analysis form at an information technology help desk may look similar to that found on the next page. Similar to the root cause analysis process, this process can also be automated. After the inhibitor is addressed, the last line on the form indicates that all the agents at the help desk should know the answer. The inhibitor analysis process itself is found on the page following the form. The root cause analysis process and the inhibitor analysis process are both required to make an environment effective and efficient. In either case, a knowledge base (departmental document repository) is updated so that solutions are known for issues. There is no need to reinvent the wheel. Both processes will reduce costs by preventing reoccurring problems and increasing productivity, communication, and customer satisfaction.

Inhibitor Analysis Form

Date Opened (mm/dd/yy): __/__/__

Name of Agent: _____ **(Last, First)**

Problem:_____
_____
_____
_____
_____
_____
_____
_____

**Inhibitor (Check One): Process/Procedure__ Hardware__ Software__
Network__ Training__ Staffing__**

Resolution/Actions (by Team Lead):
_____
_____
_____
_____
_____

Date Completed (mm/dd/yy): __/__/__

Support Desk Agents Notified: (Y/N)

Inhibitor Resolution Workflow

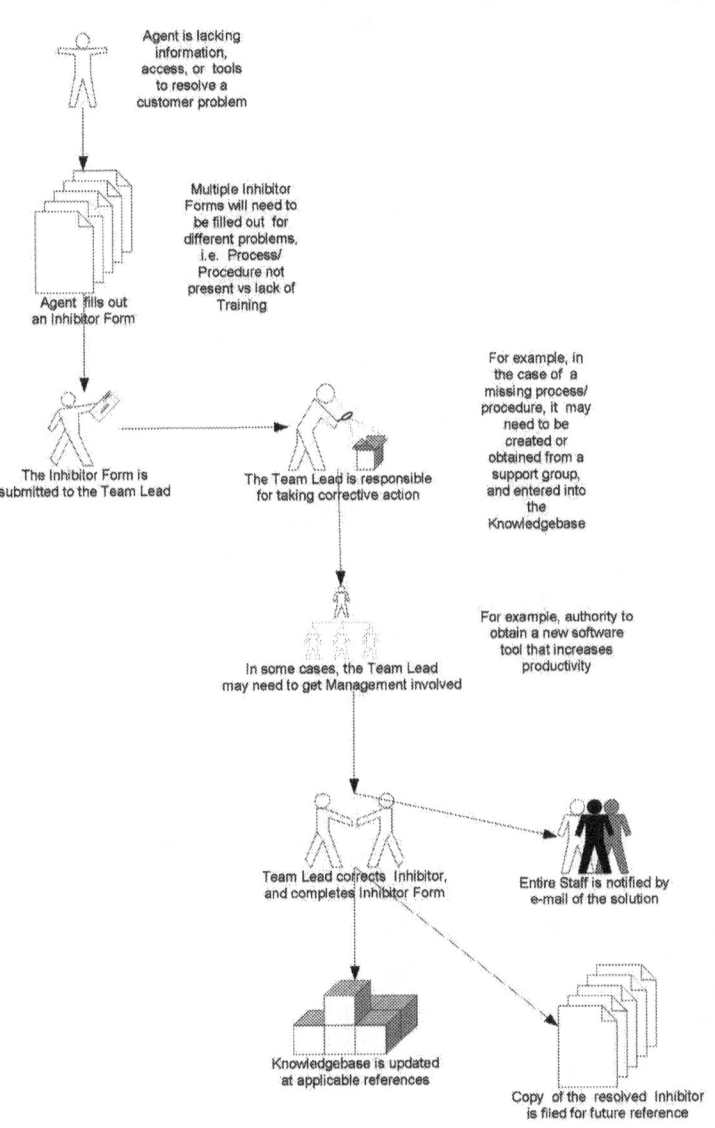

Agent is lacking information, access, or tools to resolve a customer problem

Multiple Inhibitor Forms will need to be filled out for different problems, i.e. Process/ Procedure not present vs lack of Training

Agent fills out an Inhibitor Form

For example, in the case of a missing process/ procedure, it may need to be created or obtained from a support group, and entered into the Knowledgebase

The Inhibitor Form is submitted to the Team Lead

The Team Lead is responsible for taking corrective action

For example, authority to obtain a new software tool that increases productivity

In some cases, the Team Lead may need to get Management involved

Team Lead corrects Inhibitor, and completes Inhibitor Form

Entire Staff is notified by e-mail of the solution

Inhibitors decreasing on a monthly basis indicates increased productivity for customers & employees, and also indicates that management is resolving internal reoccuring problems within a department(Operating Efficiency)

Knowledgebase is updated at applicable references

Copy of the resolved Inhibitor is filed for future reference

3. **Technology**

As mentioned earlier, organizations can realize considerable cost savings through technology, but automation also allows for ease of doing business with a company, thereby increasing customer satisfaction. Has your company implemented the following technology to satisfy both internal and external customer needs?

- ACDs (automatic call distributors) This device handles heavy incoming call volume and sends a call to the first available agent. If all agents are busy, it plays a recorded message and music and places the call in a queue, until an agent becomes available.

- Predictive dialers. This is a computerized system that automatically dials batches of telephone numbers for telemarketers.

- Speech IVRs (interactive voice response units). These respond to customer voice commands (speech recognition) for such things as password resets and customer ticket orders without human intervention (i.e. Ticket Master), or directs to the appropriate department for problem resolution.

- CTI (computer-telephony integration) software allows customer accounts to auto-populate automatically into the program used by agents who answer calls at a help desk or call center.

- Reporting software, such as Crystal Reports[22], used in conjunction, for example, with a problem-reporting tool like Remedy[23], to display statistics in a more easily readable format.

- Problem/change management software, such as Remedy or Vantive[24], that is used to keep track of problems and changes in an organizational environment.

- Scheduling software, such as TCS[25] or Blue Pumpkin[26], to appropriately schedule staff.

- Knowledge bases to archive and update documentation.

- Network devices with built-in redundancy for business continuity.

4. **Expenditures**

Organizations have to seek ways continually to minimize expenditure and maximize profits by doing such things as:

- Implementing conference calls instead of traveling to business meetings.

- Web-enabling a help desk or call center to reduce cost per call (fixed costs plus variable costs, divided by number of calls answered) through customer self-help options.

- Outsourcing a help desk or call center to India or Mexico to further reduce the variable costs (salaries, bonuses, benefits, telecomm costs) by about fifty percent.

- Use economies of scope. Use a single software program to perform a function throughout an organization, instead of using multiple types of software that perform the same function in different divisions.

- Use economies of scale. For example, have call centers in the West cover for call centers in the East due to the time difference (follow-the-sun concept), instead of hiring additional staff in the East.

- Standardize processes, practices, and technology within an organization in the manner in which an ERP (enterprise resource planning) system such as SAP[27] software does for an organization. Therefore, on the front end, a company's sales division will not sell more product than the manufacturing division can produce. Adding a company human resource module, back-end processes such as problem and change management can be tied into the scheme, so that these department functions are visible to all interacting department personnel.

- Use online faxing software such as Genifax[28] to considerably eliminate the amount of paper wasted within an organization.

- Implement root cause analysis and inhibitor analysis to resolve reoccurring problems company-wide, so resources are not continually wasted on these issues but can be directed elsewhere, for example, for the completion of projects.

- Resolve customer issues on the first call (FCR—first call resolution), to eliminate the necessity for additional staff needed when customers call back multiple times for the same issue.

- Continuously measure departmental objectives and raise the bar yearly for continuous improvement. For example, if a call center had a handle time goal of three hundred seconds per call, and they achieved this objective, next year the goal should be lowered to two hundred seventy seconds per call. This saves a considerable amount of money in head count.

- Vigorously pursue competitive strategy—operational efficiency, product leadership, or customer intimacy, as described in Chapter 2.

By analyzing, understanding, and continuously evaluating the four elements that encompass a department or corporation—people, processes, technology, and expenditures, an organization will have a firm foothold on continuous improvement and be able to operate and compete effectively.

4

A Learning Organization

A learning organization, the name for a quality management organization, so coined by Peter. M. Senge (the heir to Dr. W. Edwards Deming) in his book *The Fifth Discipline*[29] (1990) speaks about how employees within an organization should continuously learn from each other through inquiry and understanding the big picture (how what others do, tie into your job). In contrast, the traditional management philosophy believes that one can learn only from one's superiors. In fact, years ago, one of my managers actually gave me this line. This was a traditional manager who believed that power and taking direction without question, should be a way of life.

Learning is a continuous process, regardless of age. Individuals can learn from their peers, employees, superiors, strangers, customers, and family. Due to the fact that traditional managers do not believe in this philosophy, you will find that traditional organizations continuously repeat the same mistakes without resolution, because learning never takes place. You will also find that executives in these organizations make decisions from the top-down, instead of from the bottom-up, therefore, many decisions are not realistic and do not benefit these companies. A lack of organizational learning costs these companies millions of dollars every year, and hit directly at their bottom line.

We all saw some extreme cases of this traditional philosophy in 2002, when the executives of multi-national firms manipulated accounting practices to their benefit, because they had the power and influence to do so, and because they thought they were above the law. These executives should not have been placed in these positions in the first place, and once discovered, should have been removed by the boards of directors. Obviously, quality management was not being practiced within these organizations, because that comes from the CEO, and from a practice of putting corporate goals over individual agendas, a practice then conveyed to everyone within an organization.

How does an organization become a learning organization? Incorporate these practices company-wide:

1. **Initiated by Executive Management Team**—The CEO and executive management team must be willing to adopt this philosophy and make it a mandate that the entire organization will be trained in quality management practices, and then take the appropriate action to drive this behavior. An outside firm can be hired to provide this training, or it can be developed in-house and tailored to a company's specific needs. The most important point here is that the company's executive management team has to buy into this new operational philosophy and convey this message to company employees through its behavior and actions. Management should create an environment that fosters learning.

2. **Question Everything**—No matter what one's organizational level, do not take anything at face value. Do not be shy to speak up at meetings, because there is no such thing as a stupid question. Inquiry promotes learning within an organization, because others may have the same question but are unwilling to ask. However, one must always exercise the appropriate interpersonal skills. For example, if you are at a meeting, and thought that the findings that the presenter just displayed were incorrect, you shouldn't say those numbers were totally bogus, and you don't know how he or she came up with them. Instead, what should be said is something similar to this: My numbers don't match yours; can you please tell me how you arrived at those figures? Quality organizations, unlike traditional organizations, promote proper interpersonal skills to enhance organizational learning and create leaders. Nobody wants to learn anything from individuals who have no respect for others.

3. **Be a Mentor-Facilitator-Coach**—Promote organizational learning by teaching peers, employees, and superiors. Yes, I did say superiors, and that was no mistake. An individual learns best by teaching others. Everyone needs a little assistance now and then, especially those new to a department or a company. Traditional organizations typically do not show new arrivals the ropes, but rather throw them to the wolves from day one. If employees do not feel welcome, they will not be willing to stay. Also, do not assume that your management knows everything as well, because they do not. Most managers in traditional organizations get to where they are through seniority and nepotism, not because they know more than you do. Quality organizations do not accept this practice. Individuals are promoted from within based on performance and qualifications, or hired from the outside based on a variety of qualifications. Management in quality organizations expects you to make a continuous contribution for the betterment of the overall team, and may mentor you to perform projects. However, no one should have to ask for your assis-

tance. Mentoring should be done without hesitation, because you are improving overall learning within the organization. A colleague who recently went to another company said that it is very difficult to find another individual like me, who shares knowledge. Most people do not make the time to mentor others, because they consider it unproductive time for themselves, or because they think that if someone is unable to perform a particular job function immediately, he or she should not be in that position. Management in quality organizations typically requires mentoring others as one important criterion within each employee's performance appraisal. Each individual can make a contribution to creating a learning organization.

4. **Share Knowledge**—Take every opportunity to share your knowledge and work with others. As in traditional organizations, do not keep knowledge to yourself because you consider it job security; there is no such thing as job security these days. In traditional organizations, because knowledge is not shared, a new employee replacing someone who has left has to start from scratch. This is unacceptable in quality organizations. There should be a documentation database where all created files are kept for posterity. There is no need for others to re-invent a process or procedure if you already possess it. Think in terms of the productivity of the entire organization, not just yours. Do not worry about who gets the credit for work performed; the most important thing is the effectiveness and efficiency of the environment. Your colleagues, management, and employees will know who did the work. If they do not, you are working for the wrong organization anyway. Every process or procedure I have derived, I have always shared with my colleagues and management. Some wonder why they receive this information from me. They may even view it as bragging. It is my high regard for a learning organization that drives this behavior.

5. **Communicate Thoughts Clearly**—No one in the organization should have to guess what you meant in your phone message or e-mail, because it is a waste of productive time. When you communicate clearly, you are increasing the productivity of recipients within the organization, because the recipients do not have to return your phone call to get clarification, or respond with another e-mail. For example, do not forward an e-mail with just one word or one line, unless the e-mail clearly explains the communication. Do not assume just because you understood what was stated in the text of an e-mail, that the intended recipients would understand.

6. **Learn While Delegating**—A manager needs to know how to delegate to give employees the necessary skills for advancement. However, if a manager does not learn a process or product, how can employees be mentored appropriately? How can they be given appropriate performance apprais-

als at the end of the year? Managers need to empower employees, but need to learn skills themselves to grow and be effective in the workplace.

7.   **Listen More Than You Speak**—Managers can learn much from colleagues, customers, and employees. However, they will never hear the important details if they are always in the habit of telling others what to do, instead of listening. Remember, there is a big difference between hearing and listening; listening means that you comprehend what is being said. Employees can give valuable input, because they are the best at doing their jobs. Colleagues can give valuable input because they maybe outside of your present situation and see things more objectively. Customers can give valuable input because they use your services or products. Remember that it is all right to have criticism in the workplace as long as it is constructive criticism or feedback. In other words, if it is not aimed at you but at improving the overall environment, healthy debate is valuable, because it improves the result.

8.   **Challenge Yourself**—Everyone should push himself or herself to do things not done before. These unfamiliar tasks may make one feel uncomfortable at first, but in the long run will help one's knowledge and career. For example, in my early work years I was terrified of public speaking, but I knew that I had to overcome my fears if I wanted to succeed. I attended departmental meetings where I spoke about my particular information technology job function at the time, and the overall function of my department. This helped me build a relationship with other departments in my information technology division, and helped them in turn to understand and communicate better with my department. But most of all, it helped me to feel comfortable when speaking in public, which I needed at that time for graduate school. As a result, public speaking in management school was not an issue, and today I do not even think about it if I have to speak in public. When one does unfamiliar tasks it engages the learning process and makes one more effective in the long run.

9.   **Embrace Change**—You cannot turn a company into a quality organization unless the management and employees embrace change in the first place. Some will not accept change, and will either leave or will be terminated. When individuals reject change they are stating that they are unwilling to learn new skills and grow within a company. Since a company has to continuously grow and seek new methods to compete in today's market, a company cannot afford to hire or retain these types of employees. If employees do not fit into the culture, they will not be good role models or mentors for others within the company. A belief in quality management takes much more dedication than believing in traditional management values. It takes a lot of effort, understanding, and teamwork

to be successful. Candidates should not be hired into a company unless they are willing to embrace change and continuously learn new skills. This may entail wearing many hats from time to time: a leader, a follower, a teacher, a student, and a team player. The value brought to an organization is the ability to adapt to any situation or crisis. A wonderful book for an organization to read on change is, *Who Moved My Cheese?* [30] by Spencer Johnson, M.D.

10. **Understand Single Loop vs. Double Loop Learning**—Single loop learning[31] means that a company never learns from its mistakes and continuously makes the same mistakes over and over again, at a cost to the bottom line. Think of it as a car going in a circle, it never goes anywhere. An example from the information technology arena shows that the existing problem management process does not work because problem tickets are constantly closed without resolution, sacrificing productivity and customer service. However, management does nothing to rectify the situation. This typically happens in traditional management organizations. Double loop learning [32] is typically found in quality management organizations, where the same mistake is rarely made twice, because employees have learned from their mistakes and have shared this information with others. Think of it as a car that is wound up and let go within an enclosed circle. Every time it hits the circle wall, it goes in a different direction, which means that it has adapted from the acquired knowledge. In the same problem management process example above, learning will take place due to root cause analysis and inhibitor analysis, as discussed in Chapter 3, for a permanent solution.

11. **Recognize the Big Picture**—Recognize how your actions or inactions affect not only your work, but also the work of others. Peter Senge calls this systems thinking. Systems thinking represents a major leap in the way people are used to thinking. It requires the adoption of a new paradigm (discussed in Chapter 8). Although there is no such thing as a learning organization, we can articulate a view of what it would stand for. In this sense, a learning organization would be an entity that individuals would truly like to work within and that can thrive in a world of increasing interdependency and change.[33] According to Senge, systems thinking is critical to the learning organization, because it represents a new perception of the individual and his or her world:

At the heart of a learning organization is a shift of mind from seeing ourselves as separate from the world to connected to the world, from seeing problems as caused by someone or something 'out there' to seeing how our own actions create the problems we experience. A learning organization is a place where people are continually discovering how they create their reality and how they can change it.[34]

Further, systems thinking require skills and tools that can be developed only through lifelong commitment (self-mastery). Additionally, it requires that not one, but many organizational members acquire these skills. Therefore, learning organizations have come to be known also as communities of commitment.[35]

Executive management must understand the benefits of creating a learning-based culture instead of a power-based culture. The value of getting everyone thinking alike (systems thinking) and focusing on the employee and customer cannot be over emphasized, and will have a very good outcome on the bottom line. Executive management must ensure that corporate management pursues these same goals, and in turn passes them down to employees within the company. Instituting the values of a learning organization will create a more committed, productive and rewarding environment for years to come.

5

Relationship Building

Building lasting relationships internally (with colleagues, employees, management, and other departments) within a company and externally (with customers, vendors, and family) is not done well by most employees or managers. In traditional organizations, building working relationships and interpersonal skills is not emphasized, because management within these organizations do not have these skills to begin with, so how can they possibly mentor employees? Also, since traditional managers believe in using power over individuals, they do not care much about establishing and maintaining relationships.

In quality organizations this concept is given prime importance, because in order to get tasks completed within an organization, you need to rely on other departments or colleagues, therefore relationships must be forged and nurtured. Managers who build solid working relationships with their employees and empower them, can accomplish more and have a more productive staff, due to the respect that is bestowed upon them from their employees. Employees will go the extra distance to perform projects for such managers, without having to be asked. Additionally, I have worked for a number of companies that treat their contractors terribly, and do not give these individuals equal status within the company, resulting in much attrition within the environment at a great cost to these vendors. The management of these traditional organizations cannot comprehend that if they treated their contractors well, six months down the road they could hire these individuals as loyal company employees. Traditional organizations lose many talented individuals who will never work for these companies due to their reputation. Career-oriented employees, seek quality organizations where their talents are recognized, where there is opportunity for advancement, and where a learning environment exists, to establish long and successful careers. These are the types of employees desired by traditional organizations as well, but due to the nature of these environments, these individuals typically do not stay very long.

Quality organizations also build long-term relationships with customers by delighting them with their product or service. This loyal customer base continues to purchase additional products and services from these companies yearly, adding directly to their bottom line. Therefore, the goal in today's marketplace is not to sell a product or service one time to a customer, but to retain them as lifetime customers. In the case of both employees and customers, it is more cost-effective for a company to retain them rather than to replace them at great expenditure to the organization.

Shaun Smith, co-author of *Managing the Customer Experience*, outlines the reason the customer experience is so important:

The experience you deliver every day, through every interaction, direct or indirect, either builds value for your brand or destroys it. The banking industry is a perfect example. Eighty percent of customers who switch between suppliers were satisfied with their previous supplier—yet they switched. A good experience with a company can increase loyalty by 33 percent. Further, branding a customer's experience and ensuring that customers are satisfied results in loyalty, profit, and the possibility of turning customers into advocates—people willing to argue a company's case to their friends, who in turn bring in even greater profit. This makes economic sense. It costs six times more to acquire a new customer than it does to keep an existing customer. A 5 percent increase in customer loyalty increases the lifetime profits from a customer by as much as 95 percent. Investing in building loyal customers is an investment in profit growth.[36]

How can the management of an organization build lasting relationships with its employees and customers? Institute the following practices:

Employees

1. **Address Employee Concerns Promptly**—For example, if a female employee had a child recently, depending on the position, a flexible shift or telecommuting may be appropriate. If an employee is having car trouble, why not arrange to have him or her picked up? If the previous manager continuously blamed a particular employee, when in fact, it was the manager's fault, the succeeding manager has to make it up to that employee, and assure him or her that that practice has ended. I managed a Danka help desk years ago. A female manager who managed a sister help desk at another location hated one of my female employees, who used to work for her at one time. This manager took every opportunity to persecute my female employee. This ended soon after I took over as manager, and I promised the employee that I did not act in this manner. The human resources department agreed with me, stating that there was some sort of personality conflict. Traditional managers have this preconceived notion

that the employee is always at fault, instead of viewing the situation objectively. Therefore, when another traditional manager takes over the staff, the trend continues. If a manager hates his or her employees, this individual should not be in management. But as I stated in a previous chapter, many become managers without any proper training and due to seniority and nepotism. Addressing employee concerns promptly will increase productivity.

2. **Create a Non-Threatening Environment**—Be approachable, no matter what rank you possess within a company (supervisor, manager, senior manager, director, vice-president, president, or CEO). Do not wield power over employees, as a title does not make an individual better or gain the person respect. As I stated in the previous chapter, being a mentor-facilitator-coach, is much more productive for an environment. As the saying goes, you can do more with sugar than you can with a stick.

3. **Use Interpersonal Skills**—Address deviant behavior using your best interpersonal skills. Remember, every time you deal with an employee, you are being a role model. Therefore, yelling or screaming at employees in front of others is not going to accomplish your objectives. Instead, the employee is no longer going to respect you as a manager from that point forward. Your goal is to change an employee's behavior as stated in Chapter 1, without lowering the individual's productivity.

4. **Encourage Feedback**—Value employee opinions. Never reject employee ideas; rather, have them discuss the pros and cons with colleagues and have the department come to a consensus. However, if a consensus cannot be reached, the manager will have to make the decision. Do what is best for the business. If employees disagree with your decisions, they have a right to their opinions. Do not consider them the enemy. People can disagree and still get along. The best solutions are implemented by seeking out different points of view.

5. **Promote Teamwork**—Encourage employee participation in many different tasks and projects. This makes employees feel accepted and valued as members of a department. Leadership classes that promote company wide team building activities are invaluable.

6. **Have Outings Together**—Consider your employees and colleagues your second family and attend functions together on a regular basis. These should be kept strictly professional, but they can be fun too. Create a hard-working but fun environment.

7. **Never Set Employees Up To Fail**—For example, in the outsourcing industry, it is typically not a good idea to promote a team lead (supervisor) from

the existing help desk to a manager. Due to existing relationships, this individual may not be treated well by the rest of the staff. In a situation such as this, it is better to hire a manager from the outside. The team lead in this scenario should be promoted to a management position in another department or outsourcing contract.

8. **Create An Open-Door Policy**—An employee should have the freedom to approach anyone within the organization concerning a human resource issue, beyond his or her immediate supervisor. This is especially important if the issue is with one's immediate supervisor. Bypassing one's immediate supervisor is not looked at favorably in traditional organizations, and repercussions to the employee may follow. Therefore, in reality, there is no open-door policy in traditional organizations, because the employee is always told to speak to his or her immediate supervisor concerning any issue with them. The employee, fearful of repercussions, will never speak to the supervisor, and will eventually leave the company because the supervisor may continue to practice a behavior that is not appropriate. Quality organizations always emphasize an open-door policy, and there are no repercussions to the employee from the manager. Constructive feedback will be given to the manager from his or her own manager or the human resources department. Quality managers appreciate the feedback as an opportunity to learn and grow, because a certain behavior may not have been seen as wrong, but on reflection, the manager decided that it was inappropriate for all parties. Employees typically recognize quality managers, and will give them the courtesy of addressing a situation prior to escalation.

9. **Apologize When Necessary**—Quality managers use this extensively, because it goes a long way toward building relationships with employees. Traditional managers never apologize to their employees, because it is seen as a sign of weakness. Quality managers understand that apologizing to one's employees is actually a strength because it means that you care about and have respect for your employees, and that transcends any titles. Also, if you are mentoring others to be leaders, this is a very important trait to possess. Using this when appropriate, will keep the communication channels open, maintain morale, and gain respect.

10. **Be Objective**—A manager has to be fair and objective with all employees. There should not be any subjectivity where the manager sides with one employee over another, because the manager has a closer relationship with one employee. Remember, the objective here is building relationships, not destroying them. If employees recognize a manager as unfair, they will leave the company. The number one reason for employees leaving a company, as stated previously, is their immediate supervisor. For this reason, a manager should not be a friend to any employee in his or

her department. In traditional organizations, management makes it abundantly clear which employees they favor, and promote those employees, even though their work and interpersonal skills may not be as good as that of others. Quality managers recognize that for an employee to be a great leader, that individual does not have to be a friend.

In addition, as mentioned in Chapter 1, always create **win-win outcomes**. Managers who practice these behaviors will gain respect and higher productivity levels from their employees. Also, employees will go out of their way to perform extra work for such managers, and there will be less absenteeism, because it will be fun to come to work. All this results in increased revenue for a company's bottom line, because there will be less attrition and as a result less hiring and retraining. Also, due to increased productivity levels, a company actually accomplishes more with fewer resources.

Customers

1. **Customer Satisfaction**—If a customer is not satisfied at the end of a transaction with your organization in regard to a product or service, you can be assured that the customer will not return. The goal of relationship building is to maintain customer loyalty for future purchases, which can be very profitable for companies. Loyal customers tend not only to purchase more often, but also to spend more money in their purchases, than one-time customers. Corporate help desks and call centers have realized this and have started asking customers questions like the following at the end of each call: "Have I resolved all your issues today to your satisfaction"? If a customer states no, it allows a representative (because he or she is the first line to the customer representing a company) to further ensure that a customer is satisfied, prior to ending the call. It may not always be possible for a representative to resolve a customer's issue because, for example, the issue may be system-related, but at least an attempt was made, and hopefully the customer was compensated in some manner. I purchased a bed last year for my four-year-old son, and the local furniture store promised that it would be delivered in three weeks. It took the store two months to deliver the bed. I was informed that they were having some supply issues with the manufacturer. Customers do not care about internal coordination issues, only that they receive the product on time, and in the condition specified by the seller. This furniture store also did not bother to contact me and say that my product would be delayed. I had to make numerous calls to this store, and it was a real inconvenience. Needless to say, I will not purchase any more furniture from this retailer. Instead of making a loyal customer out of me (because their

prices and quality were actually very good), they made me a dissatisfied customer due to their inaction.

In Chapter 1 (Employee Champion), I mentioned that employees are the front-line to customers and represent the company. Therefore, employees have to be treated very nicely. Otherwise, they will not bother to build lasting relationships with customers, who in return, will give additional business to a company. Richard F. Gerson, PhD, president of Gerson Goodson, in his article *Seven Steps to Building Better Customer Relationships*, states that customer service reps (CSRs) in a call center or help desk environment are uniquely positioned to help a company build secure and long-lasting customer relationships, because they frequently have contact with the customer. When CSRs take the time to serve and satisfy customer inquiries (relational), there is often a measurable increase in repeat business. However, when the CSRs treat customers simply as transactions to be completed in a certain amount of time (transactional), satisfaction decreases, loyalty suffers, and repurchase behaviors decline. Therefore, it is extremely important to develop appropriate behaviors in the CSR staff to increase the mental (emotional) ties that bind customers to a business. Customers who do not like the way they are treated can easily switch to a competitor, regardless of the financial costs associated with the switch. However, when the emotional costs of switching are greater than the financial costs, then there is less likelihood that a switch will occur. On each contact, CSRs have to do everything possible to ensure that the emotional state of the visiting customer is satisfied. When a customer is bound emotionally (mentally) in addition to physically (owning the product or service), a bond is created with the customer.[37] The seven steps to building better customer relationships for CSRs are:

a. Gather Accurate and Current Customer Information—This is critical because customers want to be seen as more than a number. They want to be treated as individuals and respected. Customers want a company to know them personally and know their needs and expectations. Therefore, on every call, a CSR should initially update the customer file. However, if a customer is upset (not using a normal tone of voice), a CSR should take a moment to calm him or her down and put the customer's mind at ease, prior to gathering this information. If a customer calls with a normal tone of voice, the profile information can be gathered at the very beginning of the call. Also, asking the customer if the last time he or she called (for example, on an inquiry), if he or she were satisfied with the service and outcome, would be a good method of trying to establish the relationship.

b. Product Knowledge Experts—CSRs have to know their products, programs, and service offerings inside out. They do not need to be technical experts, although this would help. However, CSRs must be familiar with all aspects of the business, who does what, and how customers are supposed to use company products. In order for CSRs to accomplish the above, they must use company products on a regular basis themselves. A customer does not want to be transferred elsewhere because a CSR answering the phone is not familiar with what the customer is asking. Multiple instances such as this will prompt a customer to go elsewhere, straight to the competition. Ensure that CSRs are familiar with all company product offerings. If they come across as not knowing their products (for example, hesitation on the phone, or they have to call someone else), customers will not feel comfortable in buying a company's products.

c. Invest Time to Learn About Customers—In many call center environments, CSRs are too busy to get to know their customers because they are measured on handle time (the lower the better), which allows call centers to handle an abundance of calls without having to hire additional CSRs—the quantity vs. quality dilemma. The problem is that if CSRs are being measured on lower handle times, and the number of calls taken (the higher the better), then they will do everything possible to end customer calls quickly without providing excellent customer service. The true purpose of a customer call may not even be known. This in turn will make customers call back later (no first call resolution), or go to a competitor, both at a cost to the company. A CSR must be allowed to stay on the phone as long as necessary to satisfy a customer. As mentioned earlier, not only do satisfied customers buy more products, but also it is more cost effective to retain existing customers than find new ones. When CSRs satisfy customers instead of meeting quotas, they should be rewarded in the same manner as if they met quotas, because they are ensuring lasting customer loyalty and business. Behaviors that get rewarded get repeated. Therefore, a company should reward CSR behaviors that serve customers well, satisfy customers, and help build long-term relationships.

d. Provide Value to Customers on Every Contact—Whether customers call to complain, obtain information, or make another purchase, CSRs must provide some value at every interaction. This does not have to be a monetary reward for the customer. It is even better if the value is perceptual or psychological. For example, in the cellular industry, if a customer is paying for a higher rate plan than is necessary (observed by a CSR viewing the customer's minute usage history), a CSR making a point to tell a customer this lower rate plan and accompanying minutes would satisfy his or her needs better, creates added value and loyalty in a customer's mind. Also, customers must be thanked at every opportunity for their business.

e. Establish a Win-Win Partnership for Service—CSRs must be trained so that the success of calls is dependent on a collaborative effort with customers. When a CSR resolves an issue for a customer, without any involvement from that customer, you get only half the result you should have gotten. A CSR should work through a problem situation with a customer and they should jointly come up with the answer. This will result in a customer's buy-in for the solution and higher satisfaction rates, because both parties logically tackled the problem step-by-step. A customer perceives it to be a better result due to the customer's involvement. This results in more renewals and lower attrition rates for a business.

f. Reward Customer Loyalty—The reward is up to the individual business, but whatever it is, the reward must be perceived to be of high value by customers. For example, a small business can assign specific CSRs to certain customers. When a customer calls in or drops by needing help in resolving a problem or inquiry, the CSR assigned to them would assist this customer, even though any CSR could assist. This makes customers feel important, because they have their personal CSR. Also, the CSR can build a long-term relationship with the customer because he or she has an understanding of the customer's needs.

g. Communicate Regularly with Customers—CSRs should be active with their customer service. While many contact centers react to customer needs (wait until customers call or come in), a business should act and have CSRs contact customers just to see how they are doing with the company's product or service. Customers will perceive this as a very caring act on the business's part, and this will strengthen the psychological relationship they have with the business.[38]

2. **The Customer is Always Right**—Even when the customer is wrong, one cannot state this or argue with a customer. This is because the customer is purchasing the product (not you), and keeping you employed. Remember that many customers also practice traditional philosophies, because they have not been exposed to quality management. If a customer is verbally abusive to you, please request your supervisor to handle the situation. Never hang-up on a customer, use abusive language yourself, or increase your tone in an upset manner, as all this will make the situation worse. Remember that upset customers are not directing this abuse towards you personally. It is only because you represent the company, and for whatever reason, they are dissatisfied with a product or service. A manager maybe able to save a customer's business. On the other hand, if you do any one of the things I mention above, instead of letting a supervisor or manager handle the situation, your company may lose

that customer forever. But it does not end here. Remember that a customer who is dissatisfied with your company typically will tell seven other people, meaning that now your company has lost potential business from other parties as well. It does not matter if the customer was wrong, because that is not the story they will tell. It is much more cost-effective to the bottom line of a company to keep existing customers and obtain additional customers through word of mouth recommendations, than it is to advertise for new customers.

3. **Never Deceive Customers**—Always deliver what you promise, and never take advantage of customers. I moved my family from Philadelphia to Allentown in 2003. After inviting about six moving companies to give us a quote on the move, we settled on a local moving company for around 680 dollars. I thought that this sum was fair, considering the move was only an hour away. The Friday before the move, the movers contacted us and told us that they needed to be paid in cash. I thought this was all right, since I was still able to go to the bank on Saturday morning. When they arrived Saturday morning, they got me to sign about fifteen forms, making them not liable for numerous things. I did not have time to read all these forms (they plan it this way) as the movers were not going to move a thing prior to me signing, and time was wasting. After everything was packed, around noon, they drove to Allentown following my lead. We stopped at a highway fast-food place for about forty minutes and finally made it to the house around 2 PM. The movers have this policy that they will not take anything off the truck until after they are paid. The driver then proceeded to add the charges and quoted me a figure over $1,500. I told the driver that he was charging me 120 percent more than the saleswoman stated. He told me that this happens all the time. This company apparently low balls customers to obtain their business and springs this on the customers at the last minute. The driver said that he had no control over the charges, and that he would contact the owner of the moving company for consultation.

Naturally, the saleswoman was not available for contact. I had called her the previous day, and she had informed me to take out at least 800 dollars to be safe. I had actually withdrawn 900 dollars from the bank that morning. When the owner got on the line with me, I could tell that this individual was not accustomed to customer service by his attitude and tone of voice. Whereas the saleswoman was very friendly and courteous, this individual was extremely sarcastic and unprofessional. He told me that I probably could not afford to move in the first place, and now I didn't want to pay, and that he was not in the business of moving people for free. I told him that this was not the sum that we had agreed upon, and he said to me that sum was just for moving, and not for the materials. I told him that was not what the saleswoman had indicated to me, and he asked me to show that in writing. We had received a quote from the saleswoman, but in the process of moving, we had somehow misplaced the sheet of paper with the estimate. The owner said that was an estimate anyway. I told him that estimates according to the law can only go ten percent above or below the mark, not one hundred twenty percent. I also told him that the three individuals that arrived found the boxes that I and my wife had packed too heavy, so they tore them apart and used their own boxes, while charging me for the materials. He asked me if I wanted them to break their backs. I said no, I expected them to bring a dolly. He then spoke to the driver and reduced the amount to 1,100 dollars by asking the driver to bring back any good boxes. I told the owner that I did not want to pay that amount because that was still almost double what I had been quoted. Then he told me that I had two choices: I could either pay the amount due and take possession of my belongings, or they would take my belongings back with them in the truck. I decided that we had no choice at this point. I drove off to find an ATM to withdraw 200 dollars. It was a good thing that I was able to reduce the charge. The maximum that can be withdrawn from an ATM daily is 400 dollars, so I would have been out of luck, since I only had 900 dollars on me. I would have had to hire a lawyer and gone after my belongings, which would have taken several months or more. In the meantime, my family and I would have been living on the floor.

The movers were unwilling to take anything off the truck until they got paid. While I was away, the driver informed my wife that they were running out of time to move all our belongings, as they were supposed to be back at their location by 5:00 PM. If they stayed later, they said they would have to charge additional money. As a result, they would move any heavy furniture items upstairs, and the rest they would leave in the garage. I had wasted half an hour arguing with the owner, another twenty minutes trying to find an ATM, and it seems that I also paid for the forty-minute lunch for the driver and his crew for a total loss of ninety minutes. In this case, my family and I were taken advantage of by this moving company because the manager knew that there was nothing that we could do at the last moment. As a result, I could not say that I was unwilling to sign the forms that morning, because we had already given notice to the apartment complex where we lived that we were moving out. Also, we did not have any friends in the area that could help us move. Philadelphia also has a law that states that you cannot move on a Sunday, so we did not even have time to find anyone else, as I had to work the following Monday. I contacted the state attorney general's office, which has cited this company for a number of violations involving other customers as well. This type of deceptive business practice by traditional managers will eventually lead to the downfall of the company. If the owner of this moving company had told me the cost up front, I would have been glad to pay. He would have then had a loyal customer that would have recommended the company to others. Traditional corporations are their own worst enemies because they care only about making a quick buck, and not long-term relationships.

4. **Surpass Customer Expectations**—Bring a certain added value to the customer, and your business will experience long-term growth and profitability in this relationship. Some years back, I managed a Lockheed Martin outsourced help desk for Spherion Corporation. I not only achieved the service level objectives, but I performed projects for the Lockheed Martin customer, as well as writing many processes that allowed the help desk to become effective and efficient. My management did not expect me to perform this additional work, but I did it in order to expand the business. I was able to grow the business from twenty-five employees to forty-five employees, while opening up career opportunities for my staff. The customer manager was so thrilled with what I had accomplished within a year, that she eventually offered me her position.

5. **Have a Sense of Urgency**—Promptly respond to customer inquiries, whether they involve problem tickets, phone calls, e-mails, or appointments. Customers will appreciate it because it will increase their productivity. Some years back I reported to a director at CDI Corporation who never responded to my e-mails or phone calls. He was very evasive and probably very unorganized. I was glad to be laid off from that organization because he drastically affected my productivity. He was a traditional manager who did not understand that when you do not respond to someone you not only affect their productivity, but whoever else maybe waiting on them. How often have you called someone at the office concerning an issue and never received a call back? Individuals of traditional thought prioritize things according to what is more important to them, and not what is important to others or the corporation. They forget that their colleagues in the company may require this information to service external customers.

6. **Implement Customer Suggestions**—A great way to show customers that your company is listening to their concerns and addressing their needs is by implementing their suggestions. Johnson & Johnson developed the tamper proof safety cap on medicine bottles out of the Tylenol incident that poisoned a number of individuals in the 1980s.[39] This incident will be discussed further under Chapter 7—Leadership.

7. **Actively Follow-up with Customers**—For example, if a wireless carrier representative at a call center sold a customer a new cell phone, and the customer was supposed to receive it within three days, the representative should follow-up on the fourth day to ensure that the customer received

the phone in good condition and that it works properly. This sort of behavior goes a long way in building loyalty among customers. This is one way to differentiate your organization when it competes under a strategy of customer intimacy.

8. **Incorporate Customer Greetings and Closings**—Remember the days when you walked into a Blockbuster store and were greeted by a friendly hello by one of the sales associates? A customer feels good when greeted in such a manner by someone unknown to him or her. This is known as building customer rapport, which is the first step in establishing a relationship with a customer. At the end of a transaction, a customer should be thanked for his or her business, stating that your company appreciates the business. Call Centers that practice world-class behaviors typically use this statement in their closing. In life it is often the little things that people remember, and the same goes for customer service. Sales people do this quite well by sending their customers Christmas cards at the end of the year with a photo of them included, thereby reinforcing a face to a name.

Companies that practice these behaviors will build and maintain loyal relationships with customers that will allow them to be profitable and increase market share in the future. Employees will reward a company with greater productivity and long-term employment. Lower employee attrition levels will result in considerable savings to a company (avoiding the high cost of hiring and training new employees), and customers will appreciate the fact that they are dealing with the same knowledgeable employees over time, which in turn will result in customer retention. It is these types of relationships that allow companies to survive even in bad economic times.

Building lasting relationships with both employees and customers is an art that must be continuously worked on by employees and managers alike. Every situation addressed must be handled with care, keeping in mind the result of one's actions. The relationship must be maintained at all costs. If that means backing down from a confrontation for the good of the business, by all means do so. Always keep in mind the ultimate goal is the efficiency and productivity of the environment, which leads to profitability. If the communication channels are broken, nothing can be accomplished. Furthermore, these relationship-building behaviors will be effective not only in your work life, but in your social life as well.

6

Empowerment

Empowerment is the authority given to individuals by others to do things on their own. In Jan Carlzon's Book, *Moments of Truth*[40], he speaks about the importance of empowering employees to achieve superior customer service, because they are the best at performing their jobs. Jan Carlzon is the former president and CEO of SAS (Scandinavian Airline Systems), and he cites a wonderful example of empowerment:

An SAS Airline was stranded at an airport with mechanical problems for several hours. The flight attendant had already served the customers the regular snack and drink within the first hour. At the start of the second hour a customer approached the flight attendant and asked for an additional snack and drink. This was unheard of; there was no precedent to serve the customers a second snack and drink. Jan Carlzon calls this a moment of truth. Whenever a customer confronts an employee with a question or issue, the employee's reaction at that moment determines whether the company keeps that customer or loses that customer forever. The flight attendant asked the head flight attendant whether she could serve an additional snack and drink and was told that was against policy. She received the same message from the pilot. The flight attendant then took it upon herself to go downstairs to the SAS counter, and ask if they had any additional snacks and drinks, and was told no. She then took money from petty cash, went over to another airline counter and purchased snacks and drinks for all the customers, brought it up and served them. This is what Jan Carlzon calls customer service. He said that you cannot teach this type of customer service and promoted the flight attendant to a management position within the company.[41]

If SAS were a traditional organization, management would have fired the flight attendant. Also, the company would have lost a number of passengers as repeat customers. This outside-the-box thinking is very important for world-class customer service. Rules reflect company guidelines, but it is impossible to develop a guideline for every situation. World-class customer service and retaining customers comes down to good judgment on the part of each employee, because they are the first line of contact for the customer. Quality organizations foster empowerment in their employees in the following manner:

1. **Create a Non-Threatening Environment**—Traditional organizations defuse empowerment and creativity with the use of power and micro-management. Imagine a scientist trying to invent something in a traditional environment; it will not happen, because creativity and empowerment are stifled. Such things as creativity and empowerment flourish in quality organizations because employees are given the freedom to pursue their interests and encouraged and supported by their management.

2. **Let Employees Resolve Problems**—Guide employees to think critically for themselves and resolve issues, instead of you as a manager providing the answer. Companies require employees that can act independently. As an example, as a manager, you asked a number of employees to work on a project and report back to you weekly. If during this meeting, every time an employee gave feedback, you said that was incorrect and it has to be done this way instead, you are not empowering your employees to act on their own. This is actually traditional management behavior disguised as empowerment because you had asked them to work on this project by themselves. Better solutions will result when employees act on their own, because they are the experts at performing their jobs, and the manager may not have all the facts.

3. **Allow for Mistakes**—Companies and individuals learn and grow by making mistakes. Throughout history, many new products have been discovered, either by making mistakes or by accident, for example, the discovery of penicillin by Sir Alexander Fleming in 1928[42]. Support employees even after they have made mistakes. The most important thing is the learning that takes place within an organization. Encourage each employee to share information with the team. Individuals do not have to make mistakes on their own to learn; instead, they can learn from the mistakes of others.

4. **Never Ignore Employee Suggestions or Ideas**—One of these ideas may turn into a multi-million dollar business for the company. For example, a chemical engineer developed 3M's famous Post-It Notes.[43] If an idea is not appropriate, discuss the rationale with the employee. At least, the employee will not feel ignored by management.

5. **Develop Each Employee Through Projects**—By making each employee the team leader on a certain project, it will give each employee the confidence to grow and become an excellent contributor within the company. I once had an employee who did not need to be told anything. He would

perform many projects on his own. I was surprised when he informed me one day, that years before he was not like this at all. He was only concerned with whatever work he was expected to do, and did not get the big picture of how his contribution affected the entire organization, until a previous manager had a discussion with him. All he needed was a little encouragement, and now he encourages others to be all that they can be.

6. **Create Opportunities for Development and Advancement**—Excellent contributors need to feel valued. They require additional work for stimulation and opportunities for quick advancement; otherwise they will leave the company.

7. **Employee Recognition**—Recognize employees who have empowered themselves to provide world-class customer service, both individually as well as in front of their peers and the company. A perfect example is the SAS story mentioned at the start of this chapter. It is important to be able to emulate this behavior throughout the company. Many companies give trips to Hawaii to their best performers as well as providing recognition throughout the company. Traditional organizations, on the other hand, tell their employees that they are lucky to have a job.

8. **Create a Competitive Team Environment**—New ideas will flourish in this type of environment, and allow a company to be more competitive. Competition usually brings out the best in employees. Also, it is healthy for employees to have goals—for example, the desire to be employee of the month or employee of the year. For some employees, empowerment comes from within; others will require a little nudge.

9. **Decision Making Should Be Decentralized**—Decision making should be left to the employees and managers closest to the customer experience, and not to the CEO and senior management staff, as in traditional organizations. In the SAS example above, the flight attendant, most likely saved a number of customers for the company that day. Also, executives may not have all the details of what is transpiring to be able to make day-to-day decisions, and they really should not have to. This is because they should be dealing with the big picture issues or company strategies. If executives had to deal with day-to-day activities as well, they would be working twenty-four hours a day, and they would not need managers. Executives need to be able to rely on the management staff reporting to them to do the right thing for employees and customers alike.

Empowerment cannot be over-emphasized, as it is one of the building blocks of a quality organization. Society encourages babies and adolescents to explore and learn, but at the same time, this mindset is often lost when we turn into adults and start work. Companies need to allow their employees at the lowest levels to tap into that creative potential once again, and this is exactly what quality organizations empower employees to do. The day of the top-down organization has passed. Today's quality organization is bottom-up oriented, thereby having a pulse on customer needs and expectations.

7

Leadership

If you read Webster's dictionary, the definition of leader maybe found as an individual who leads others through influence. [44] In other words, leaders or managers influence their employees, peers, and superiors in order to obtain their objectives. Quality managers take this one step further and influence these parties to follow in a beneficial direction for the common good. Traditionally, it has been an unwritten corporate rule, that in order for one to lead in corporate America, it helps to be tall and good-looking. However, for any organization following this philosophy, it is a fallacy. Men such as Napoleon Bonaparte and Mahatma Gandhi, may not have had either characteristic, but had an enormous following and rose to the highest pinnacle during their lifetimes. My belief is that true leaders come to the forefront due to necessity. For example, Franklin Delano Roosevelt during the U.S. depression of the 1930s. However, it is personality, character, and desire to succeed that make them stand out and achieve great things, not height and good looks.

In modern times, personality traits outweigh every other advantage, and separate quality managers from traditional managers. These personality traits allow quality managers to have a loyal following, achieve desired objectives, and increase corporate profits. If an organization desires to hire and retain quality managers, then that organization needs to seek these types of behaviors from their managers and those who desire to be managers:

1. **Respect for the Individual**—Employees within an organization must have respect for those within and external to an organization—for example, vendors. Others do not have to think as you do for you to get along and accomplish common objectives. Even if parties disagree on certain practices, agree on what is best for the customer. You do not have to like someone, but you must respect that person's opinion and be able to get along, otherwise, each other's work will suffer. Traditional managers could care less about respecting others, since everything is based on power. These managers then wonder why they can never accomplish

anything. In Chapter 5 (Relationship Building), this concept is a pre-requisite to creating a win-win outcome.

2. **Keep Promises**—Making promises simply to accomplish one's objectives and reneging on them later, is not going to make one popular with colleagues, employees, and superiors. Unfortunately, this has become second nature to traditional managers. I have seen instances where a manager promised an employee a raise, and then left for another position without submitting the paperwork.

3. **Integrity and Ethical Conduct**—Never change a story in front of different people within the organization just to make yourself look good. I have personally had managers tell me something, five minutes later change the story, and the following day, say something drastically different in a meeting. Also, never knowingly do anything illegal or unethical. Integrity and ethical conduct are extremely important in business relationships as they are throughout life, and should never be compromised under any circumstances. Never give anyone a reason not to trust you. Here is an example of what unethical practices can do to a corporation:

    The Manville Corporation used asbestos since the 1930s for home and business insulation, because the mineral was fireproof. The company knew that asbestos caused cancer from the very beginning, but denied it to the public. The corporate management philosophy was to hide facts from the public. The company filed for bankruptcy protection in the 1970s when the truth leaked out and numerous lawsuits ensued. The company created a trust and paid lawsuit damages for thirty years. The Manville Corporation no longer sells asbestos products, but would not have gotten into trouble and had to restructure if stakeholder interests (management, employees, customers, owners, community) were considered from the very beginning.[45]

4. **Take Responsibility for Own Actions**—Traditional managers always find someone else to blame when something goes wrong. Quality managers will always take responsibility for their actions, because this is a trait of a true leader. Here is an example of what ethical practices can do for a corporation:

    Johnson & Johnson's Tylenol Crisis in 1982. Seven individuals died by consuming Extra Strength Tylenol, which was laced with cyanide. Jim Burke, CEO of J&J at the time, stated that the company would take responsibility, no matter who had placed cyanide in the bottles. J&J removed all Tylenol capsules from the market, citing public safety. J&J lost millions of dollars as a result. Extra Strength Tylenol, the leading pain killer medicine with a thirty-five percent share of a 1 billion-dollar market, dropped quickly to a seven percent share due to the crisis. However, out of this crisis the tamper proof cap was invented. Due to the concern that J&J had shown in the marketplace, Extra Strength Tylenol regained its market standing by surpassing the thirty-five percent it had held earlier. J&J had shown its concern for the consumer and won.[46]

5. **Ability to Apologize**—As mentioned in Chapter 5 (Relationship Building), the ability to apologize is a strength, not a weakness.

6. **Sense of Urgency**—As mentioned in Chapter 5, responding to phone calls, e-mails, and attending meetings in a timely manner shows that you are a responsible individual, regardless of whether you are dealing with internal or external customers.

7. **Give Credit where it is Due**—Do not take credit for what your employees do. Traditional organizations believe that an employee needs to make the manager look good, and the manager, in turn, when promoted, will promote the employee as well. Somehow, things do not always end up this way for an employee within a traditional organization. Quality managers take every opportunity to give credit where credit is due. They do not need to go out of their way to make themselves look good, because that will be a natural outcome when employees achieve high performance levels and there is no attrition, adding directly to the bottom line. Quality managers believe that their success will come out of making people around them succeed.

8. **Do Not Emphasize Titles & Offices**—Employees are much more at ease and can accomplish more in an environment that does not emphasize titles. As mentioned in Chapter 4 (A Learning Organization), quality managers are mentors, facilitators, and coaches. Therefore, one thing managers can do not to emphasize their title is to have cubicle offices among their employees, and not be hidden away in some office. If this is done, not only will they gain the respect of their employees (because managers will be seen as equals, and not superiors), but they will have a pulse on what is transpiring within their department, because these managers will be able to see and hear what their employees are experiencing, which is very valuable if they need to change standing policies and procedures quickly. Managers can always arrange a meeting in a conference room for any private discussions with employees. Japanese management believes in having cubicles on the center of the floor, because this is where the action is found. In fact, having a corner office means that a Japanese manager has been ostracized from the crowd. This is because the Japanese do not like to stand out (teamwork is emphasized over individualism in Japanese society) from the crowd as seen in the fact that men like to wear the same color suit. Whether one is an employee, manager, senior manager, director, vice-president, president, or CEO of a

company, one should all receive the same level of customer service from an internal perspective. If this is not the case, are we sure that our employees are treating our external customers appropriately? Quality managers typically will not include a title when they send out an e-mail, simply because it should not matter, and also because they like to build a personal relationship based on their first name with employees.

9.   <u>**Must Possess Excellent Interpersonal Skills**</u>—Most managers I have encountered do not have very good interpersonal skills, or they seem to lack them whenever they deal with employees. At the same time, the employees are the individuals in the company who perform the real work, not the managers, so they must be treated very well. As mentioned by my example in Chapter 1 (Employee Champion), you can gain much more productivity and loyalty from your employees by listening to them, and not judging them from the very start.

10.   <u>**Communication and Presentation Skills**</u>—Exceptional managers have great communication and presentation skills. They have the ability to hold the crowd in their grasp, and explain things at a level anyone in the organization could understand. Ronald Reagan possessed this ability when he was president of the United States. It is an art to be able to create a vision and spread it among the staff.

11.   <u>**Ability to Meet Deadlines**</u>—It is very important to have follow-through at work in meeting deadlines, because if one does not have this trait, it will affect the productivity of others within the organization, customer service, and the timeline for a product to market.

12.   <u>**Lead by Example**</u>—Never expect employees to do something that you are not willing to do yourself. This is a characteristic possessed by great generals such as Douglas McArthur. One will gain much more respect from employees if this behavior is practiced, instead of saying, Do as I say, not as I do.

13.   <u>**Continuous Improvement**</u>—As mentioned in Chapter 3, this is a necessity for business survival as well as expansion and profitability. This requires finding individuals who are highly motivated and who do not settle for simply performing their regular job duties, but perform projects that will make the company more competitive. These managers desire creativity, challenge, and accomplishment.

14.   <u>**Relationship Building**</u>—As mentioned in Chapter 5, this concept is very important in order to influence parties and accomplish tasks within an organization. Influencing must be done without intimidation. Good judgment and negotiation skills must be used at all times.

15. **Great Attitude**—Managers must possess this trait, as employees will not want to follow someone who is always negative or does not have the ability to give them a morale boost when they are feeling down. A work environment must be a fun place for employees to spend their time daily, and the attitude of management sets the stage for this type of environment.

16. **Problem Solver**—Employees will be looking to their management for direction in resolving issues, therefore managers have to be good problem solvers. In today's highly competitive world, this requires outside-the-box thinking to get an edge over the competition. This type of thinking, also known as a paradigm shift will be discussed in Chapter 8. Quality managers have the ability to guide their employees to think for themselves instead of giving them the answers. Traditional managers seem to ignore these issues altogether and prefer to blame employees later.

17. **Do Not Manage Strictly by the Book**—Many managers I have noticed, never deviate from corporate policies. But corporate policies cannot be written for every situation, so common sense should be your guide. For example, in a call center environment, if an agent uses up all his or her vacation and sick time, do not give this individual a verbal or written warning due to a family emergency. Those are beyond anyone's control, and one cannot plan for them. Put yourself in this employee's shoes and think how you would feel under a similar circumstance. The only advantage you presently have is that you are exempt (salary), instead of being non-exempt (hourly); therefore, you can afford to take time off, regardless. However, possibly sometime in your career you were hourly and experienced a similar circumstance. Also, every situation has to be judged by its own merits. There are employees who definitely take advantage of the system by finding loop-holes, but one cannot automatically judge everyone by the actions of a few. Employees have to be trusted and treated like adults, until they prove otherwise, or why were they hired in the first place? Managers must care about their employees and see them as human beings, not commodities.

18. **Consider Failure an Opportunity to Learn**—**Not to blame**. No one is perfect, and employees will make mistakes from time to time in the workplace. Quality managers allow for mistakes because everyone can learn from these mistakes, not just the individual who made the mistake. The important thing is that individuals learn from their mistakes, and that they do not reoccur. If employees do not learn from their mistakes and continuously make the same mistake, that should not be tolerated by management.

19. **Employee Development is Emphasized**—Continuous education should be emphasized for everyone within a company by management, as this will

greatly improve each employee's ability to get promoted to other positions, as well as enhance the employee's value to the organization. As mentioned in Chapter 1 (Employee Champion), managers should set up development plans for employees. Career pathing (creating career plans within an organization for employees to move from one job to another, and the education and experience necessary to get there) is a means of holding on to exceptional employees and managers.

20. **Open Door Policy Encouraged**—Quality management companies will also place this principle at the forefront of employee avenues. There are times, for whatever reason, when employees will have personality conflicts with their immediate supervisors. These employees need to be able to take their concerns to a higher level without the fear of reprisal; otherwise, attrition will result. I would encourage managers to be aware of what their supervisors are doing, because sometimes, even the well-meaning ones, may not be handling situations appropriately, resulting in voluntary or involuntary attrition. Traditional organizations typically will not let employee concerns get to the next level, even though they say that they have an open door policy.

In addition to the characteristics mentioned above, leaders should be employee champions (Chapter 1) and customer champions (Chapter 2). It is extremely important that managers have all these characteristics, because they are mentoring their employees for leadership some day. Traditional employees turn into traditional managers, whereas quality employees turn into quality managers. As the old saying goes, you reap what you sow. If employees are treated as mentioned above, in turn, they will treat customers to world-class customer service, and the company will be the beneficiary. Companies have to realize that employee needs have to be satisfied first, and that in turn takes exceptional leadership.

Let me mention a few things now that do not exemplify leadership but are practiced by traditional managers, and should never be used. My management practiced the following behaviors at some of the previous companies where I was employed:

1. **Fabrication of Information**—Management treated employees terribly while making themselves look good. The management staff would fabricate information on employees and write them up when they did absolutely nothing wrong. They felt that writing fallacies down on paper somehow made them legitimate. They knew that employees really had no recourse but to quit. The problem was that this company hired twenty-eight to thirty year olds as senior managers. They had no real management experience. Therefore, everything they did was based on

power and the traditional management philosophy. I was powerless to do anything, because they were my superiors. Reporting them to the human resources department did absolutely nothing, because the company consisted mostly of traditional managers. As a result of my management's behavior, there was about 150 percent turnover at a help desk that I rebuilt from ninety-five percent turnover, because it was a new contract. I put in eighty hours a week for a number of months to make it a success. We were able to meet and exceed our customer service level agreements until my management started playing various blame games.

2. **Management by Exception**—This means that management never calls employees to see how things are going or to tell them what a great job they are doing, until something goes wrong. At this point in time, they will call and blame the employee without having all the facts. Employee relationships are never solidified. This behavior is very destructive to an environment. Another example of this is office visits dedicated to digging up dirt. Traditional managers never catch their employees doing anything right, with the exception of employees that have that traditional management mindset. Traditional managers may even do this to ruin the careers of outstanding employees.

3. **Purposely Being Unclear**—This technique is used by traditional managers when they give an employee an assignment, but do not present them with all the details or the purpose of the assignment (because they themselves do not know), for blaming purposes later.

4. **Blaming Employees for Management Mistakes**—Quality managers never do this, but rather always protect employees from being blamed for events beyond their control. When I worked for one company, a senior manager asked me to send an employee home one time because he did not show up for work, and did not call to say that he would not be at work. As a result, being the manager, I had to cover that shift. This was not a good situation, because it was an outsourcing contract, making things highly visible to the customer. The employee had traded shifts with another employee and failed to show. The site manager and senior manager both neglected to ask the human resources director if an employee who does not come in for overtime (which was mentioned to my management by me) can be subjected to disciplinary action? In this case, the employee was sent home for a day without pay. When the human resource department informed my management that sending an employee home without pay for an overtime situation was not legal, I was blamed.

5. **Self-Fulfilling Prophecies**—This means that management sets the conditions for something to go wrong, and when it does, they blame the

employee. Most people may never experience this type of situation during their entire work career because this is extreme traditional behavior. You will probably think I am making this up, but unfortunately it was real.

I was made the manager of an outsourcing contract that experienced ninety-five percent turnover. It was a mainframe, network and desktop environment. I had to hire thirty employees and train them. The problem was that this help desk received about eight hundred to a thousand calls a day through voice and e-mail. The first several months, I worked eighty hours a week, and was on-call constantly. All I did the first two months was to run from employee to employee, answering questions, because everyone on the phone was new to the environment. I knew the environment from having worked there previously. Most people would have quit, but it became a personal goal for me to take a totally chaotic situation and restore structure by being able to meet customer service levels within a three-month period. I did it, which felt great at the end, because I had achieved a personal goal, but of course my management took all the credit because it was a traditional company.

Often customers in this mainframe environment (a powerful multi-user computer capable of supporting many hundreds or thousands of users simultaneously) would call and say, I am stuck in a transaction within this application, please release me. Some employees at the help desk would cycle the customer's node (a network address that identifies a customer's connection to a application) from the network, instead of going into the application and releasing the node safely. Performing this type of release would break that transaction's connection to the application, but it would still be running in the background, in what we refer to in information technology circles as a ghosted state (a transaction that is inaccessible to anyone, but still running in the background). The problem was that this transaction would run in the background within an application for several weeks before the customer discovered it. By that time, it had cost the customer thousands of unnecessary dollars because no one was using the transaction all that time.

My management's solution was to inform the entire help desk that they would be fired if this customer issue were handled in this manner in the future. Next they informed the help desk that I would be answering every question, which was an impossible task. Whenever calls arrived and a number of employees raised their hands simultaneously, I would ask which ones involved a customer stuck in a transaction, so that those issues could be handled with care.

Now imagine a situation in which I had the day off, or I was in the men's room and an employee received a transaction call, and it was handled inappropriately. Two weeks later, the customer would come to my management and inquire what happened. My management would go to a particular employee and ask, who helped you with this issue? The employee already fearful of being fired would say my manager did. This is what is known as a self-fulfilling prophecy. Many of you have probably experienced similar situations under a traditional management structure.

If a company seeks to be profitable and expand market share, then it needs to hire, develop, and retain leaders who use the quality management principles mentioned in this chapter. These managers in turn will instill quality management values within the organization by mentoring, facilitating, and coaching their employees. The return on investment (ROI) may not always be measurable, but will have a positive effect within the work environment for all parties.

8

Paradigm Shift

A paradigm shift [47] refers to thinking outside-the-box (creative thinking, and challenging conventional thought). We all have our own paradigm or what we consider reality of the world. At one time, people thought the world was flat, until proven otherwise. It is said that in order to improve on a product, one must say to oneself, if I were to build this product from the ground up, how would I do it? The reasoning here is that if one took an existing product and tried to improve on it, one might be locked into an existing paradigm—product design, feel, and operation. The inventor of the Segway human transporter, Dean Kamen, would never have invented this product if he did not think outside-the-box. Many opportunities can be lost if existing paradigms are not broken. Here is one such example that was very costly to the inventor:

Everyone knows that the Swiss invented watches. But how many of you know that the Swiss also invented the quartz watch? They did in 1967. But when the inventor introduced the watch to the Swiss marketplace, it was rejected. The marketplace did not consider it a watch because it did not look like a regular watch, have moving parts, or tick like a watch. The inventor turned around and sold the rights to the Japanese. The rest, as they say, is history, because the quartz watch turned out to be a billion dollar industry. [48]

Think about what happens, when you apply for an open position. Let us say, for example, it's a senior call center manager opportunity. If you never had the title of call center manager, you may not be able to land such an opportunity, even though you have had the title of help desk manager, and the same experience. Being familiar with both positions, I can tell you that both positions are pretty much the same. For example, the agents are measured by the same criteria—handle time, abandon rate, customer satisfaction surveys, average speed of answer, first call resolution, productivity rate, and quality assurance of calls. However, hiring managers do not see the experience of both positions as similar. The reason is that hiring managers are locked in to the existing paradigm of operational job title. However, the best indicator of performance is not your job title but your previous performance. Hiring managers need to change their paradigm and look at the added value that is brought to the opportunity by an individual who, for example, had been a help desk manager. The added value in this case is a high technical competency, process and procedure expert (for example in problem and change management mentioned in Chapter 3—continuous improvement), and possibly a higher level of motivation, based on the individual. All this will never be recognized under the existing paradigm of job title, and therefore a previous help desk manager candidate will not even be given an interview. Hiring managers are foregoing opportunities to take continuous improvement to a higher level. Salary was not taken into consideration in the example above. There are always budget constraints when hiring candidates. A decision has to be made whether you want a more experienced candidate that can take a position to the next level, but will demand more salary, or are you willing to settle for someone that would simply perform the job within the specified salary guidelines. If I were the hiring manager I would spend more for a quality candidate, rather than regret later.

Traditional managers may also use certain criteria within a resume as a barrier to entry, instead of thinking outside-the-box. For example, how many of you have been told at an interview that you have only managed a hundred employees, and not five hundred; therefore, you are not qualified for a director opportunity? From a quality management perspective, the question should be, how much attrition have you had or what value did you create within the organization? Instead, traditional managers care more about how many employees were managed. If you were managing five hundred employees, you certainly would not be managing them alone, but rather through a number of managers and supervisors. I guess the question is, if an individual is not able to manage fifty employees appropriately, would managing five hundred employees, consisting also of supervisors and managers, make any difference? Also, how many of those directors that were hired really worked out the way an organization thought they would? Unfortunately, traditional managers do not think in this manner and need to break their paradigm for the benefit of the organization.

How do organizations instill outside-the-box thinking among its employees? Consider incorporating the following within the work environment:

1. **<u>Create a Critical Thinking Culture</u>**—Participate in departmental brainstorming sessions to resolve problems or improve efficiency. Encourage employees to always think about ways to improve current processes and procedures and reduce departmental costs. For example, using Genifax[49],

an online fax system, as mentioned in Chapter 3 (Continuous Improvement) can considerably reduce costs due to the amount of paper saved.

2. **Instill Curiosity and Questioning of Existing Products/Practices**—Why do products have to look, feel, and operate the way they do? Consider the Segway human transporter example mentioned previously. Why can't we change a process that has been the same for the past twenty years? We live in a service oriented culture (United States and other first world nations). Therefore, modern technology has made it possible to accomplish things immediately instead of having to wait hours. For example, when you call a help desk, you should be able to have an application password reset immediately using an IVR (interactive voice response unit) or by a help desk agent. Previously, the help desk may have had to assign a ticket to a support team, where your password may not have been reset for hours. These days, everything is about productivity and time savings. As they say, time is money.

3. **Emphasize that Knowledge is Never Wasted**—Employees and managers should learn as much as possible about their work environment, even if something may not fall under their present job description. Traditional employees will say, that is not their job, and walk away, even if offered as a developmental opportunity by management. These employees do not understand that by agreeing to perform various duties within a company, they are expanding their horizons and making themselves invaluable and accessible to future opportunities that arise. Money is not everything. Knowledge is a reward in itself.

4. **Employees Must Understand the Big Picture**—This means not only how their particular job function effects their department, but company profitability as a whole. A company's upper management setting a vision for a company, and developing stretch goals each year, which are then passed down to the lowest levels of the organization, would be one approach to accomplishing this objective. For example, the senior vice-presidents have yearly goals that in turn are used by vice-presidents, directors, senior managers, managers, supervisors, and employees to establish their own, depending on what their direct supervisor's objectives are for a given year. This ensures that a company is in-sync in understanding the yearly objectives and acting upon them for competitive purposes.

5. **Applaud Creativity**—Employees should derive creative solutions for resolving problems. For example, Toyota Motor Corporation invented the JIT (just in time) manufacturing process in 1972.[56] The company needed to have enough parts available in stock to make the automobiles that were in high demand. The method at the time was to stock boxes with various parts in rows, and when the workers reached a certain box, the label read,

order more of this part. The result is today's EDI (electronic data inter-change) technology used in local supermarkets, where scanners automatically recognize product prices and deducts each item from existing inventory. Each product is re-ordered when the existing inventory reaches a certain threshold.

6. **Emphasize Working Smarter, Not Harder**—This is especially important because workloads are increasing due to job cuts and job consolidations. For example, any departmental reports that are manually run should be automated to save time daily.

7. **Encourage Thinking of Solutions, Not Costs of Implementation**—Even though some solutions are cost-prohibitive, thinking of costs first would prohibit employees from deriving the best solution. Remember not to forego correct processes and procedures due to a lack of staffing. When I was hired into a help desk management position at Danka Corporation, I found that the help desk was performing hardware fixes. Customers had Lantronix boxes (communication devices to Unix systems) that they were sending to the WAN (wide area network) team to fix, because they were not working. The WAN team did not have sufficient staff to perform this task. Since these customers were calling the help desk and complaining, the previous help desk manager had decided to let the help desk employees perform this task. However, this customer service solution by the help desk was not addressing the real issue, which was the WAN department's lack of staffing, and their responsibility to perform this function. Also, the help desk was creating a disservice to other customers who did not have hardware issues, because they were calling the help desk and waiting in queue for lengthy periods of time.

I informed the WAN manager, that if my help desk agents were busy troubleshooting hardware issues, a customer who wants to open a critical severity ticket could be delayed for half-hour or more. Also, I declared that this critical issue might be something that the WAN department needed to resolve, but it would be delayed in doing so under the present conditions. This is basic systems thinking[51] that each department or function has to do its part. Otherwise, it will affect the efficiency and reputation, in this case, of the information technology division as a whole.

However, the WAN manager, being traditional in nature, did not really care to understand or make any corrections. He informed me that he did not have enough staff, and I told him that had nothing to do with implementing the correct process. Unfortunately, because the senior manager at the time was unwilling to reverse this decision, I had to live with it. The senior manager was a quality manager, but he wanted all the managers to come to a consensus on every decision. Since that hardly ever happens among management, many issues went unresolved. In situations such as this, the leader needs to step in and make the appropriate business decision for the good of the customer. It is not good to be too much of a quality manager (believing in consensus), otherwise, there will be no improvement in the environment.

8. **Teach Staff to Solve Multiple Problems Simultaneously**—Solutions to problems do not have to be derived individually. For example, a supermarket has a parking problem (not enough parking spaces for its customers) as well as a theft problem in the neighborhood. Relocating to another location may resolve both issues.

9. **Revisit Solutions Semi-Annually**—Processes should be reviewed every three to six months because what was appropriate at one time may no longer be appropriate today. This is why it is very important that every process incorporated within a company has process owners. Otherwise, departments may be following outdated processes that will have a detrimental affect on customer service.

10. **Encourage Employees to Voice Opinions**—Many employees are reluctant to do this around management; however, constructive discussions are good for generating new ideas and solutions. Management should give fair consideration to every idea generated by employees within a department as well as give them the opportunity to be heard.

To be profitable in today's marketplace, companies will continuously have to invent new products and new methods of doing business. Therefore, every employee should be encouraged to think outside-the-box. An example is T-Mobile's (wireless carrier) hot spots [52], where business travelers can access the Internet, e-mail, and their work files through a wireless connection while enjoying a cup of coffee at Starbucks.

Occasionally, this paradigm shift is brought about by government action due to consumer demand, as in the Wireless Local Number Portability Act[53], which was mandated for wireless carriers on November 24, 2003. This act essentially stated that wireless carriers must provide the means for customers to keep their existing phone numbers when moving from one carrier to another or relocating to another area or state. This applies when customers move from wireless to wireless, wireless to landline, and landline to wireless, initially in the major markets, later to be throughout the U.S. This made it especially convenient for sales people, because they do not have to continuously print business cards when changing territories, saving individuals and companies ongoing expenses. It also made for a more competitive market among wireless carriers where customer service will be imperative in keeping existing customers and securing new ones for some time to come.

9

Task Force

A team is a group of people who get together to achieve a common goal, in which the success or failure of the team is determined by each individual's contribution coming together flawlessly with other member contributions to achieve the desired objective within a specified time. As the word implies, **T**ogether **E**veryone **A**chieves **M**ore. Each member maybe an expert at a certain specialty but needs the knowledge or talents of the collective to successfully accomplish an objective. The whole in this case, is worth more than the individual parts.

Consider all the accomplishments in sports and at work that are accomplished by teams. Even though there are many types of teams (sports teams, planning teams, steering committees, developmental teams, etc.), I will examine a team that is very beneficial to an organization, known as a task force—a team that gathers for a short period in time to complete a project and then disbands after this objective has been accomplished. Quality organizations use these teams very successfully to achieve desired objectives. Traditional organizations say that they believe in teams, but in the end, a manager will make a decision that overrides any work accomplished by a team. Whether a task force is created to address attrition within an organization, to resolve system problems, to re-write job descriptions, or to re-evaluate processes and procedures, organizations can make the time spent within a task force more productive by incorporating the following practices:

1. **<u>Membership Selection</u>**—Members have to be selected who desire to be on a team, and should not be arbitrarily appointed. The reason for this is that each member needs to make a contribution, and members will not do so unless one gets their buy-in. When I worked at CDI Corporation as a senior manager, the vice-president I reported to created a task force to alter site manager versus project manager job descriptions (there was one job description for both, even though they were two separate roles), and appointed me as the lead. He selected other senior managers to be on this team, without consulting them in advance. The result was that these

other senior managers would not perform any work, stating that they were too busy, and would only attend the meetings on occasion. Since the vice-president had set a deadline for the project to be completed, I performed ninety-five percent of the work myself. I could not approach the vice-president and tell him that these others were not doing their part because I needed to maintain working relationships with them. Also, the vice-president only cared about getting the task completed, not everyone's participation, because he was a traditional manager. This type of situation will not foster future involvement in task forces by any of the participants, because they never volunteered, but were directed to participate by a superior.

2. **Members Must Have Expertise**—When a task force is created to address an existing issue, it maybe necessary to involve members not only from one department, but members from a variety of cross-functional departments. This is because often, the individuals in one department will not have the required expertise to resolve the issue. For example, if it was suspected that slow response time within applications was caused by some sort of network issue, then this task force should include members from the LAN (local area network), WAN (wide area network), desktop support, operations, and application support teams. The individual creating this task force may actually reside on a totally different team, such as a help desk. The important thing to remember here is that each member should be selected because he or she is an expert in a field, and not simply because the person wants to be on a task force.

3. **Competent Task Force Leader**—This is important because this individual has to ensure that the objective is accomplished within a certain time, without excuses. In the CDI Corporation example above, the task would not have been completed on time if I had not taken individual responsibility to complete it, even though I was thrown into that situation. This will not be the case in most situations. Even though I was appointed to be the task force lead, I had already bought into it (in my mind) and realized that it was a necessity. Quality managers will ask individuals instead of appointing them, because if the leader does not buy into accomplishing a task, he or she could not convince others to do so. The leader should be given the opportunity to select interested parties, who are also experts in their field, because this individual has a vested interest in completing the assignment. Traditional managers simply use their power to get a task completed; otherwise the appointed leader will suffer the consequences.

4. **A Clearly Defined Objective**—This is important because the task force has to be productive during its meetings and also needs to meet a deadline. Therefore, whoever championed this task force (sponsored it),

should give a clear definition of what needs to be accomplished, so the task force does not go outside its scope. In the example above, it was to come up with separate job descriptions for a project manager versus a site manager, and the accompanying compensation structure. However, the vice-president did not say to address the reporting structure in each case. If the team had decided to do that on their own, it would have been clearly outside the scope of the task.

5. **Set A Deadline**—The given task will never be accomplished in a timely manner if a due date is not set. But the deadline has to be realistic in terms of the task that needs to be accomplished. This will be an extra assignment for individuals on the task force, so their time constraints in terms of workload have to be considered during the member-selection process.

6. **Team Must Be Self-Managed**—A manager who championed this task force should give direction only if it is getting away from the stated objectives. Otherwise, the creative juices of the team members should be allowed to flow. Traditional managers find this a difficult proposition, but they may be compromising some ingenious solutions.

7. **Manager Must Meet with Task Force Members Weekly**—This is mainly for a manager to understand the progress of a task force, and ensure that any obstacles are removed that prevents the task force from accomplishing its task within a given time. It also shows that a manager is actively participating in ensuring that the employees and the project succeed.

8. **Remove Non-Contributing Members**—This should be done by the task force lead. Those who have the interest and talent should replace these individuals to help this task force succeed. However, this situation may have been avoided from the start if team members were asked to join instead of being forced to join.

9. **Incorporate Findings**—No one wants to be on a task force in which decisions are made, but in the end, the manager ignores the findings and makes his or her own decisions. Managers should value the time, effort, and thought that went into completing a project. These findings should be valued and incorporated, because it came from the employees, and they are the best at performing their jobs. It is also very important that the individuals who plan the effort, are the ones implementing it. In the CDI Corporation example, the senior managers who managed the site and project managers were those who planned the change in job description, as well as the ones implementing it. However, if an outside consulting firm had completed this project without any involvement from company

senior management, there would not be any buy-in to implement the changes.

10. **Recognize The Team**—A task force should be recognized and celebrated for accomplishing an objective. In some cases, these task forces save companies hundreds of thousands of dollars every year by researching and resolving problems, as in the slow response time issue mentioned above. In these situations, the team deserves company recognition as well as some award. Traditional organizations may consider this part of an employee's job duties and may not recognize the effort that has been put forth by the team.

Quality organizations will continuously use and empower task forces to identify and resolve pressing issues within the environment. This is especially true for reoccurring problems that cause dissatisfied customers to move to the competition. Task forces can bring much added value to a corporation and help corporations manage more effectively and efficiently, which adds directly to the bottom line.

10

Corporate Goals, Not Individual Agendas

Quality managers practice the E-C-O concept discussed in Chapter 1 (Employee Champion) at all times. They understand that if they do right by employees, the employees in turn will do right by customers, and the organization will achieve success; also, profits will rise, the stock price will increase, and the company will gain market share from the competition. In a nutshell, this means that employees are valued as the front line to customers and that ethical behavior will lead to profitability. There is no such thing as a part time quality manager; one either is, or is not. These individuals practice the behaviors mentioned in this book at every opportunity, so that it becomes second nature to them.

This behavior is also incorporated into the family lives of quality managers. There is no distinction between the way these managers behave at work, and the way they behave at home. One cannot separate the family life from the work life. It is always a balance, but one has to take care of one's family life to be successful at work. Otherwise, one will always be thinking of what is happening outside of work, and therefore work time will not be productive. This is why quality managers will not expect employees to come to work when they are sick, because they care about employee well-being and also realize that their time at work will be less productive. Also, these sick employees could infect other employees with their germs, and now many employees are out sick, increasing a company's lack of productivity, which is costly. Employees also appreciate the caring that quality managers show their employees, and will be loyal to these managers, thereby lowering absenteeism and attrition rates.

Traditional managers place individual agendas ahead of corporate goals. They couldn't care less about the company, as long as they achieve their objective: to climb the corporate ladder. These individuals will step on anyone in the way of their objective. Employees are viewed simply as a means to achieve their goals.

Typically, their management will not see this behavior (unless employee satisfaction surveys are conducted), because traditional managers tend to act one way towards their management and another way towards their employees and customers (both internal and external).

These managers will give employees a hard time when sick and will still expect the employees to be at work. Employees who do not even have a history of constant absenteeism will be treated badly. This then leads the employee to acquire a bad impression of the company and results in attrition at a later date. These managers want their employees at work to show the company that they do not tolerate absenteeism, and that they run a tight ship. However, traditional managers are missing the big picture, and the effect that their behavior has on their employees. Employees cannot do anything right around traditional managers. If employees do not perform, they are fired (as it should be). However, if employees are exceptional workers, they too maybe fired or bypassed for promotions, because they are considered a threat to the manager's standing within the company. Employees will not be loyal to these managers, and will create heavy absenteeism and attrition within the company, because they know these managers do not care about their welfare.

Traditional managers do not understand or practice the E-C-O concept. Unethical behavior is considered a means to an end. The problem with this type of environment is that employees are mentored in the wrong behavior, thereby creating a culture that is corrupt, where only traditional management behavior is accepted. However, the result will be that the company will not succeed and be profitable, and may even get sued and go bankrupt. Given a choice between doing the right and ethical thing versus doing the political or unethical thing, traditional managers will always choose to do the political or unethical thing. Therefore, this behavior is very destructive to an organization and these individuals should be removed from management.

Quality managers understand that if they make people (employees, colleagues, managers and customers) successful around them, they in turn will get promoted, and there is no need to stab people in the back or do the political thing in order to climb the corporate ladder. Therefore, they concentrate on corporate goals over individual agendas. It is not just a matter of one individual becoming successful within an organization, but rather everyone has to be successful in order for a company to be successful.

Quality managers also believe in finding the right fit for an opportunity because this behavior gives a company a competitive edge over the competition, especially if some individual hidden away in some department happens to be a guru in a certain discipline. Traditional managers believe in protecting their colleagues and promoting individuals who act like them, even if these individuals accomplish nothing for the business, thereby bypassing an individual who would have taken a particular role to the next level.

Traditional managers do concentrate on doing whatever is necessary to make the stock price rise, and if they need to use unethical behavior, so be it. Unfortunately, this is partly due to the way American corporations work—they care only about short-term objectives and profits, unlike their Japanese counterparts that concentrate on long-term objectives and profits. Traditional managers feel the pressure to show a profitable balance sheet every quarter.

Quality managers understand that corporate goals are not simply about stockholders, but about "stakeholders"[54]—the welfare of the employees, customers, managers, stockholders, and the surrounding community must be considered. Several years ago when Enron faced legal trouble because of unethical business practices, it was not just the stockholders that suffered. The employees lost their jobs, the managers who had no involvement with unethical dealings lost their jobs, energy prices went up for Enron's customers, the stock price decreased for the owners (stockholders), and the surrounding community lost economically because money was not being spent by laid off Enron employees. Consider the two totally different outcomes mentioned in Chapter 7 (Leadership), when stakeholder interests were considered (Johnson & Johnson), and when they were not considered (Manville Corporation). The traditional managers at the Manville Corporation thought they were simply cheating the public, but in fact, the company had to pay hefty lawsuits and fines, and their reputation was damaged forever.

When you think about it, does it make sense for traditional managers to think of their own self-interests over that of the welfare of the corporation? I would argue no. These days for breaking the law, these unethical executives will be prosecuted to the fullest extent of the law, their life savings will be taken away, they will spend time in jail, their families will be disgraced, they will not be able to obtain credit in the future, and most will never be able to work for another company. Crime may seem to pay at the moment of the transaction, but in the long run it does not.

Interestingly enough, I believe one of the reasons these traditional managers get into trouble, other than their personalities (they have a God like complex, thinking that they are untouchable and above the law), is that they are able to separate their work and family life. They can act one way at home, and a totally different way at work, thereby disguising their white-collar crimes. However, they do not consider the effect that all this has on their own family, because again they put their own individual goals, over the family's well-being. This behavior does not promote long-term success.

However, the above scenario is for traditional managers who get into legal trouble, and not the ones who practice unethical behavior daily, no matter how minor it may seem. An example would be selecting a candidate for a position internally, and still going through the motions of interviewing others for the opportunity. Even if another candidate were perfect for the position, were the most qualified, and interviewed the best, he or she would still not land the position. This is because corporate unethical behavior, unless some law is broken (as is the case when defrauding stockholders under the guidelines of the Securities & Exchange Commission), is not considered illegal, although it may be highly unethical. Corporate human resource departments view this as favoritism, but not illegal behavior. Unfortunately, these loopholes encourage unethical behavior on the part of traditional managers.

How can managers be taught corporate goals, not individual agendas? It all starts with a company's mission statement. The best example I have ever encountered is Johnson & Johnson's Credo[55], which is depicted on the next page. This sense of responsibility carried J&J through the Tylenol Crisis in the 1980s and allowed it to do the right thing. Notice that the credo states that if J&J does the right thing by their customers, employees, and surrounding community, the stockholders (owners) will benefit. With a credo such as this, it does not matter who is running the company, all must live by these words. In 1943, when General Johnson outlined the four areas of responsibility, he set the framework for the company for generations to come.

OUR CREDO

We believe our first responsibility is to the doctors, nurses and patients,
to mothers and fathers and all others who use our products and services.
In meeting their needs everything we do must be of high quality.
We must constantly strive to reduce our costs
in order to maintain reasonable prices.
Customers' orders must be serviced promptly and accurately.
Our suppliers and distributors must have an opportunity
to make a fair profit.

We are responsible to our employees,
men and women who work with us throughout the world.
Everyone must be considered as an individual.
We must respect their dignity and recognize their merit.
They must have a sense of security in their jobs.
Compensation must be fair and adequate,
and working conditions clean, orderly and safe.
We must be mindful of ways to help our employees fulfill
their family responsibilities.
Employees must feel free to make suggestions and complaints.
There must be equal opportunity for employment, development
and advancement for those qualified.
We must provide competent management,
and their actions must be just and ethical.

We are responsible to the communities in which we live and work
and to the world community as well.
We must be good citizens—support good works and charities
and bear our fair share of taxes.
We must encourage civic improvements and better health and education.
We must maintain in good order the property we are privileged to use,
protecting the environment and natural resources.

Our final responsibility is to our stockholders.
Business must make a sound profit.
We must experiment with new ideas.
Research must be carried on, innovative programs developed
and mistakes paid for.
New equipment must be purchased, new facilities provided
and new products launched.
Reserves must be created to provide for adverse times.
When we operate according to these principles,
the stockholders should realize a fair return.

This sense of corporate responsibility has once again allowed Johnson & Johnson to be included in Fortune Magazine's "2005 America's Most Admired Companies" list.[56]

Conclusion

Quality managers are not born; they are guided and mentored to believe in the principles of quality management outlined in this book. If corporations truly want their managers to concentrate on corporate goals, not individual agendas, they must hire the correct management staff and train these individuals in quality management by declaration of the CEO. It will create a culture and philosophy second to none, and will allow a corporation to succeed even in bad economic times. The E-C-O concept (Employee—Customers—Owners) cannot be over-emphasized and will have a positive effect on company profits and market share. I have not gone into graphs and charts in this book for simplicity, but if you do not believe that quality managers can increase corporate profits and market share through their behaviors, then I would ask you to read *Good To Great* by Jim Collins.[57] I did not include such material in this book because the average individual who goes into management does not tend to read books at the graduate school level. However, at the same time, they are interested in learning principles that will help them manage more effectively. Also, I did not want to make this book very lengthy, because I wanted it to be carried around at all times as a reference guide, and not to be kept on a shelf collecting dust.

In today's competitive world, an understanding of quality management is vital to a company's survival and success. I hope I have been able to paint a picture of the type of behavior required to be a quality manager, and the ensuing long-term benefits for the corporation. I wrote this book because in my twenty years of employment, I have seen traditional managers do some very destructive things to the corporate environment, and yet very few corporations recognize it.

Many of the suggestions I have provided within this book are common sense, and yet practiced sparingly if at all by corporations. It is not enough for a few individuals or a division within a company to practice these quality principles, which is equivalent to not practicing them at all. Management must live and breathe these principles, to be able to mentor others appropriately. In order for this to occur, the entire corporation has to adopt this management philosophy.

Individuals will also come to the realization that they cannot separate their work life from their family life. These principles if practiced, will have a positive effect on one's family life.

This book was written for those who desire to be quality managers, but did not have the proper mentoring. It was also written for colleges and graduate schools who teach quality management, but did not have a management text-book that depicted the different behavior patterns between the quality and traditional management styles. It was important for me to prepare graduating students in these differences, because they are taught quality management theory in college, but discover after they graduate that most companies in the real world practice traditional management. If this book persuades college students to become quality managers and traditional managers to switch to quality management, it has been well worth writing.

Glossary

Word or Phrase	Definition
Abandon rate	The number of customer calls that dropped because their call was not answered in a timely manner, divided by the total number of calls received for a day, turned into a percentage.
ACD	Automatic call distributor—a device that handles heavy incoming call volume and puts a call to the first available agent. If all agents are busy, it plays a recorded message and music and places the call in a queue until an agent becomes available.
ACD time	A customer service representative's time on the phone with a customer.
ACW	After call work time—The time a customer service representative spends completing a customer request or ticket after the call has ended.
Added value	Customers look for this criterion when purchasing products and services from a company, and include such things as freebees, rebates, quality, price, reputation (branding), doing more than is contractually obligated, world-class customer service, fewer defects, options, and resale value.
ASA	Average speed of answer—how fast a help desk or call center will answer a customer's call.
Asset management	A process and software used by information technology departments to keep track of who has existing assets such has PCs, printers, monitors, laptops, fax machines, plotters, etc.
Blue Pumpkin	Staff scheduling software by Blue Pumpkin Corporation, a division of Witness Systems Corporation.
Branding	A company's reputation or logo.
Call Center	Central locations for high-volume customer calls, where questions about products and services are answered. Typically, for external customers.

Word or Phrase	Definition
Callbacks	Customer service representatives calling customers back for resolution on issues.
Career pathing	Creating career plans within an organization for employees to move from one job to another, and the education and experience necessary to get there.
Carpe diem	Seize the day, and enjoy the pleasures of the moment.
Cell tower	A cellular phone signal transmitting location.
Change management	A process and software used by information technology departments to submit new hardware or software changes or fix existing problems within a company, without impacting the production (customer) environment.
Competitive edge	A certain expertise or added value that gives a company an advantage over the competition, such as being the lowest cost provider, innovations, product and service differentiation, or excellent customer service.
Continuous performance appraisal	Manager meets monthly or quarterly with each employee to determine if measurable objectives are being met in order to determine a particular rating at the end of the year.
Cost per call	The yearly cost of customer phone calls entering a help desk or call center, measured by: variable costs plus fixed costs divided by number of calls answered.
Cross-docking	When a company does not keep inventory and re-orders supplies area-wide for multiple stores at the same time, that are picked up by trucks at a central location and delivered to the stores.
Crystal Reports	Reporting software by Business Objects Corporation that is used in conjunction with problem reporting software such as Remedy, to display statistics in a more easily readable format.
CSR	Customer service representative—an individual who answers customer inquiries at a call center or help desk.
CTI	Computer telephony integration—software that allows customer accounts to auto-populate automatically into the program used by agents who answer calls at a help desk or call center.
Customer intimacy	Employees being very courteous, helpful, and knowledgeable when customers seek assistance in their shopping experience in order to build a loyal customer base.

Word or Phrase	Definition
Customer satisfaction survey	A survey given periodically by a company to customers to determine the customer experience when purchasing products and services from the company, in order to improve the quality of products and services offered.
Development plans	A process by which management develops each employee's skills and contributions to the organization to promote them to the next level.
Disaster recovery (continuity management)	A process and plan initiated and tested periodically to protect existing assets, personnel, and the business from disasters, such as hurricanes, floods, tornadoes, fires, bombs, etc.
Double loop learning	The same mistake is rarely made twice, because employees have learned from their mistakes and have shared this information with others.
E-C-O principle	Quality management concept that states if you treat employees well, they in turn will treat customers well, resulting in loyal customers who will continue to purchase products and services from a company. This in turn, will increase company profitability, stock price, and market share, resulting in making the owners (stockholders) happy, because they will realize increased returns. A term that summarizes the behavior of quality managers.
Economies of scale	In this context means taking advantage of available resources to reduce costs, as in a call center in the West covering for one in the East during the latter hours of the day.
Economies of scope	In this context means to use one software to perform a function throughout an organization, instead of using multiple types of software that perform the same function in different divisions.
EDI	Electronic data interchange—A technology that allows a device such as a scanner to read product prices and re-order inventory when available supplies reach a certain threshold, to meet consumer demand.
Employee satisfaction survey	A yearly employee survey conducted by an organization to determine how the work environment can be improved.
Empowerment	The authority given to individuals by others to do things on their own.

Word or Phrase	Definition
ERP system	Enterprise resource planning system—An integrated set of applications that ties all the departments within a company to one central view, thereby for example, preventing the sales division from selling more product than manufacturing can produce. SAP is an example of such a system.
FCR	First call resolution—resolving a customer's issue on the first call, so the customer does not have to call back.
Focus group	A meeting with customers to gather their needs, suggestions, and satisfaction levels, as well as having customers try out new products and services.
Follow the sun concept	Instead of hiring more staff in a call center in the East as the day turns into night, have the call center in the West cover after a certain time, which helps contain costs.
Gap analysis	The state of processes today versus where your organization wants to be, and what will be done to reach the desired state, or close the gaps.
Genifax	Online fax software by Omtool Corporation.
Ghosted state	A mainframe application transaction that is inaccessible to anyone, but is still running in the background.
Handle time	The length of time it takes a help desk or call center to complete a customer call.
Help desk	A central location where customers call for assistance on information technology issues—computer related questions and problems. Typically, smaller than a call center, and mainly for internal customers.
Help desk agent	The name given to customer service representatives who answer help desk calls.
Hot spots	Locations where business travelers can access the Internet, e-mail, and their work files through a wireless connection while enjoying a cup of coffee, for example at Starbucks.
Inhibitor analysis	The front-end (proactive) process for resolving employee inhibitors, to be able to effectively service customers.
IT	Information technology—the term used for the computer field or a computer department.

Word or Phrase	Definition
ITIL	Information technology information library—a process designed for information technology departments that covers all the process disciplines required to manage this area effectively, such as problem, change, and asset management, among others.
IVR	Interactive voice response unit—a company's 1-800 number (systems that provide recorded messages over the phone in response to user input) for customer contact and call routing to the appropriate department.
JIT	Just in time—designed by Toyota Motor Corporation to have enough available parts when manufacturing cars. Today, this process is used as EDI (Electronic Data Interchange) technology in scanners at supermarkets and other stores.
Knowledge base	A company's or department's documentation depository that keeps answers and solutions to customer requests and problems, updated regularly.
LAN	Local area network—a company's internal network.
Land lines	Home telephone service.
Leader	An individual who leads others through influence, in a beneficial direction, for the common good.
Learning organization	The name for a quality management organization, so coined by Peter M. Senge in his book *The Fifth Discipline* (1990). The concept that employees in any organization should constantly share knowledge, learn from inquiry, and understand the overall goal of the department and company (the big picture).
LIFO	Last in—first out—in this context means the employees that are hired last are released first during a layoff.
Mainframe	A powerful multi-user computer capable of supporting many hundreds or thousands of users simultaneously.
Management by exception	This means that management never calls employees to see how things are going or to tell them what a great job they are doing, until something goes wrong. At this point they will call and blame the employee without having all the facts. Employee relationships are never solidified.

Word or Phrase	*Definition*
Market-driven economy	Consumer demands have to be met, otherwise, they will take their business elsewhere. Customer demand determines what products and services merchants offer.
Market niche	Companies need to compete within their field of expertise, sometimes in a small market segment, in order to be profitable.
Merchant-driven economy	Customer either buys what a merchant sells, or goes elsewhere. Merchants determine what they want to sell.
Moment of truth	Whenever a customer confronts an employee with a question or issue, the employee's reaction at that moment determines whether the company keeps that customer, or loses that customer forever. So coined by Jan Carlzon, former President and CEO of Scandinavian Airline System in his 1987 book, *Moments of Truth*.
Node	A network address that identifies a customer's connection to an application.
One-on-one	A monthly or quarterly employee-manager meeting to discuss performance, career aspirations, concerns or suggestions on the employee's part, and in general how things are going.
Open-door policy	A corporate policy by which employees can surpass their immediate management and take issues to any level within the organization without suffering any repercussions.
Operational excellence	A company uses its infrastructure as a competitive weapon.
Outsourcing	Transferring the non-core business of an organization to an outside vendor, to realize considerable cost savings to the bottom line.
Paradigm shift	Thinking outside-the-box and challenging conventional thought.
Predictive dialers	A computerized system that automatically dials batches of telephone numbers for telemarketers.
Problem management	A process and software used by information technology help desks to document, escalate, and resolve customer-affecting issues.
Product leadership	Companies that invent products and continuously strive to beat their own standards and be the market leader.
Productivity rate	Available Time plus ACD time plus ACW time plus callbacks minus lunch, divided by 6.5 hours, put in a percentage.

Word or Phrase	Definition
Qualitative	The interpersonal skills aspect of management—how well employees, customers, colleagues, vendors, and other managers are treated by management personnel.
Quality assurance departments	A department that monitors agents or CSRs in a company for quality compliance on customer calls, such as customer greeting, correct problem diagnosis, FCR, appropriate documentation within the customer ticket or record, customer closing, and tone of voice.
Quality manager	A manager whose behavior is summarized by the (ECO) employees—customers—owners principle.
Quantitative	The measurements aspect of management.
Rate plan	A cellular customer's contractual agreement with a company that includes such things as the price per month, the number of minutes per month, whether it is an individual or family plan, whether the plan includes nights and weekends, whether the plan is a local, regional, or nationwide plan, and how much additional a customer will pay per minute when all the minutes are used.
Relational	The concept that customer service representatives take the time to serve and satisfy customer inquiries, and build relationships with customers.
Remedy	Problem management software by Remedy Corporation, a division of BMC Corporation.
Renaissance employees	Employees that have the skills and motivation to perform in a variety of positions.
ROI	Return on investment realized by a company by instituting some new technology and the time period in which the investment will pay for itself.
Root cause analysis	The backend (reactive) process for resolving customer issues permanently, so that they do not reoccur.
Self-fulfilling prophecy	In this context means that management creates the conditions for an employee to fail, and then blames the employee.
Server	A hardware device that is networked and allows multiple customers to process requests or get work done. A PC can be used as a server, depending on the number of customers using its services, its available memory, and processor speed.

Word or Phrase	Definition
Single loop learning	Means that a company never learns from its mistakes, and continuously makes the same mistakes over and over again, at a cost to the bottom line.
Six sigma	Means seven errors per million. Initially derived by Motorola Corporation to reduce manufacturing costs through various processes and procedures. Present day it is also used in business departments to reduce reoccurring problems through black belt programs.
SLA or SLO	Service level agreements or service level objectives—Internal company measurements or external contractual obligations that have to be met for customer satisfaction.
Speech IVR	A company's interactive voice response unit (1-800 number) with voice recognition technology for customer contacts and call routing to the appropriate department. A customer would speak in natural language instead of choosing an option as is done on a regular IVR.
Stakeholders	Individuals that either benefit or suffer from corporate actions—employees, customers, managers, stockholders, and the surrounding community.
Succession planning	The process by which employees are mentored to take another employee's position due to promotion or attrition.
Systems thinking	Understanding the big picture and how the work of one individual or one department affects another.
Task force	A team that gathers for a short period in time to complete a project, and then disbands after this objective has been accomplished. Depending on the issue, it could be a cross-functional (intra-departmental) team.
TCS	Staff scheduling software by TCS Software Corporation.
Thinking outside-the-box	Creative thinking, and challenging conventional thought.
Traditional manager	A manager whose behavior is summarized by power, fear, and control (micro-managing) employees.
Transactional	The concept that customer service representatives treat customers simply as transactions to be completed in a certain amount of time. This behavior does not build lasting customer relationships.
Vantive	Problem management software by People Soft Corporation.

Word or Phrase	Definition
Virtual reps	Websites that have animated assistants that help answer customer inquiries through online chat by accessing a knowledgebase. They are programmed to continuously learn from their customer interactions.
WAN	Wide Area Network—a company's external network.
Win-win outcomes	When dealing with anyone—customers, colleagues, managers, employees, strangers, or family, it is important to create a situation where both parties walk away from the conversation feeling good about the events that just transpired, because it is important to build lasting relationships.
Wireless local number portability act	Initiated on November 24, 2003, this act stated that wireless carriers must provide the means for customers to keep their existing phone numbers when moving from one carrier to another or relocating to another area or state. This applies when customers move from wireless to wireless, wireless to landline, and landline to wireless, initially in the major markets, later to be throughout the U.S.
World-Class customer service	Ability to meet and exceed customer service level agreements for measurements in ASA, FCR, handle time, abandon rate, productivity rate, quality of the call, system uptime, customer satisfaction surveys, etc.
Zero defects	A concept used by the Japanese in manufacturing, meaning no defects, or perfection when making products.

Endnotes

1. Thomas J. Peters and Robert H. Waterman Jr., <u>In Search of Excellence</u> (New York: Warner Books, 1982), 1–325.

2. Jan Carlzon, <u>Moments of Truth</u> (New York: Harper & Row, 1987), 1–135.

3. Peter M. Senge, <u>The Fifth Discipline</u> (New York: Doubleday, 1990), 1–390.

4. "Welcome to Motorola University", n.d., <u>https://mu.motorola.com</u>, (January 2004).

5. "Just-in-time manufacturing (JIT)", n.d., <u>http://concise.britannica.com/ebc/article?eu=394102</u> (January 2004)

6. Tim Marks, "Zero Defects", 7/18/03, <u>http://healthcare.isixsigma.com/dictionary/Zero_Defects-550.htm</u> (January 2004).

7. "The 100 Best Companies To Work For", <u>Fortune Magazine</u>, (January 24, 2005), 61–90.

8. "The 100 Best Companies To Work For", <u>Fortune Magazine</u> (January 12, 2004), 61.

9. "Stew Leonard's Farm Fresh Foods", n.d., <u>http://www.stewleonards.com/html/about.cfm</u> (April 2004).

10. The Associated Press, "Wal-Mart Tops Fortune 500 List", 4/4/2005, <u>http://www.cbsnews.com/stories/2005/04/04/national/main685527.shtml</u> (April 2005).

11. Michael Treacy and Fred Wiersema, <u>The Discipline of Market Leaders</u> (New York: HarperCollins, 1995), 1–204.

12. <u>The Discipline of Market Leaders</u> (New York: 1995).

13. "The 100 Best Companies To Work For", <u>Fortune Magazine</u>, (January 24, 2005), 62–68.

14. "Testimony of Mr. Danny Wegman", n.d., http://edworkforce.house.gov/hearings/107th/21st/wia91202/wegman.htm (March 2004)

15. "The 100 Best Companies To Work For", Fortune Magazine (January 24, 2005), 73.

16. Thomas J. Peters and Nancy K. Austin, A Passion For Excellence (New York: Warner Books, 1985), 66.

17. The Discipline of Market Leaders (New York: 1995).

18. "2005 America's Most Admired Companies", Fortune Magazine, (March 7, 2005), 67–82.

19. "Southwest Airlines:The Hottest Thing in the Sky",(Most Admired Companies) Fortune Magazine (March 8, 2004), 86.

20. "Verity Completes Acquisition of NativeMinds Inc", n.d., http://www.verity.com/products/response/new/ (January 2004).

21. "The ITIL and ITSM Directory", n.d., http://www.itil-itsm-world.com/ (January 2004).

22. "Business intellignece that works for you", n.d., http://www.businessobjects.com/ (January 2004)

23. "Business Service Management from BMC Software and Remedy", n.d., http://www.remedy.com/ (January 2004).

24. "PeopleSoft", n.d., http://www.vantive.com/corp/en/public_index.jsp (January 2004).

25. "TCS Software", n.d., http://www.tcssoftware.com/ (January 2004).

26. "Manage to Excellence with Blue Pumpkin Workforce Optimization Solutions", n.d., http://www.bluepumpkin.com/ (January 2004).

27. "Innovative Solutions to Innovate Business", n.d., http://www.sap.com/ (January 2004).

28. "Accelerated Document Routing for today's office", n.d., http://www.omtool.com/ (January 2004).

29. The Fifth Discipline (New York: 1990).

30. Spencer Johnson, M.D., Who Moved My Cheese?, (New York: G.P. Putnam's Sons, 1998), 1–94.

31. Chris Argyris, <u>Overcoming Organizational Defenses</u> (New Jersey: Prentice Hall, 1990), 92.

32. <u>Overcoming Organizational Defenses</u> (New Jersey: 1990), 94.

33. Fred Kofman and Peter M. Senge, "Communities of Commitment: The Heart of Learning Organizations", American Management Association (1993), 32.

34. <u>The Fifth Discipline</u> (New York: 1990), 12–13.

35. "Communities of Commitment", <u>American Management Association</u>, (1993).

36. Sarrah Norris & James Hall, Quality vs quantity", 6/13/03, <u>http://brw.com.au/smearticle.asp?doc_id=22677&dcat=20001</u> (May 2004).

37. Richard F. Gerson, PhD, Seven Steps to Building Better Customer Relationships", n.d., <u>http://www.mailsbroadcast.com/2003.CRM.Ezine/Ecrm.0203.Htm</u> (May 2004).

38. Richard F. Gerson, PhD, Seven Steps to Building Better Customer Relationships", n.d., <u>http://www.mailsbroadcast.com/2003.CRM.Ezine/Ecrm.0203.Htm</u> (May 2004).

39. "The Tylenol Crisis: How Effective Public Relations Saved Johnson & Johnson", 1/1/98, <u>http://www.personal.psu.edu/users/w/x/wxk116/tylenol/crisis.html</u> (February 2004).

40. <u>Moments of Truth</u> (New York: 1987).

41. <u>Moments of Truth,</u> (TV Special, 1988).

42. "A Science Odyssey: People and Discoveries", n.d., <u>http://www.pbs.org/wgbh/aso/databank/entries/bmflem.html</u> (January 2004).

43. "Science & Technology: Sticky Notes", 4/5/04, <u>http://pubs.acs.org/cen/whatstuff/stuff/8214sci3.html</u> (May 2004).

44. "One Look Dictionary Search", n.d., <u>http://www.onelook.com/</u> (October 2003).

45. Joseph W. Weiss, <u>Business Ethics</u> (CA: Wadsworth, 1994), 2–270.

46. <u>Business Ethics</u> (CA: 1994).

47. <u>Moments of Truth</u> (New York: 1987).

48. "The Quartz Watch Inventors", n.d., http://www.si.edu/lemelson/Quartz/inventors/swissinvent.html (February 2004).

49. "Accelerated Document Routing for today's office", n.d., http://www.omtool.com/ (January 2004).

50. "Just-in-time manufacturing (JIT)", n.d., http://concise.britannica.com/ebc/article?eu=394102 (January 2004).

51. The Fifth Discipline (New York: 1990)

52. "T-Mobile Hot Spots: U.S. Locations", n.d., https://selfcare.hotspot.t-mobile.com/locations/viewLocationMapForLocationDomain.do (November 2003).

53. "Wireless Local Number Portability: FCC Consumer Facts", n.d., http://www.fcc.gov/cgb/consumerfacts/wirelessportability.html   (December 2003).

54. Business Ethics (CA: 1994).

55. "Johnson & Johnson: Our Credo", n.d., http://www.jnj.com/our_company/our_credo/index.htm;jsessionid=K1UHV4R1SSHHWCQPCCGSZOYKB2IIQNSC (January 2004).

56. "2005 America's Most Admired Companies", Fortune Magazine, (March 7, 2005), 67.

57. Jim Collins, Good To Great (New York: HarperCollins, 2001), 1–210.

978-0-595-35756-7
0-595-35756-3

www.ingramcontent.com/pod-product-compliance
Lightning Source LLC
Chambersburg PA
CBHW030819180526
45163CB00003B/1355